MW01068196

Sonita

Sonita

My Fight Against Tyranny and My Escape to Freedom

Sonita Alizada

HarperOne

An Imprint of HarperCollins*Publishers*

The names and identifying characteristics of some of the individuals featured throughout this book have been changed to protect their privacy.

HarperCollins books may be purchased for educational, business, or sales promotional use. For information, please email the Special Markets Department at SPsales@harpercollins.com.

harpercollins.com

FIRST EDITION

Designed by Kyle O'Brien
Photographs courtesy of the author

Library of Congress Cataloging-in-Publication Data has been applied for.

ISBN 978-0-06-343900-9

25 26 27 28 29 LBC 5 4 3 2 1

To Rokhsareh, who believed in my voice.

To Nana, my mother, for her love and for choosing me over traditions.

To you, for unfolding my story and allowing my words to be heard.

Contents

Prologue

"Can you buy me?" I asked the Iranian filmmaker who had been documenting my life for three years. Now, it seemed her protagonist was about to be sold into marriage. What a terrible ending for a documentary.

"You have six months before your wedding," my mother said.

Enough time to plan my escape.

1

War and Hope

"Why are you smiling, Sonita?" Latif, my older sister, asked me quietly. She didn't want to interrupt Baba, my father, who was praying from the Quran out loud as if God had fallen asleep. I cannot fully recall how many times Baba begged Allah to stop the war that visited us more often than God himself.

Bang! Bang! As the bullets were released, one after another, our dead, dark basement came to life, my family's hearts beating faster than the heart of the mighty war in the corner of our neighborhood. Baba cried God's name repeatedly, without even thinking that maybe God would not pay us a visit because it was curfew time, or maybe he did try to come to rescue us but the Taliban shot him for breaking their rules. After all, Afghanistan could not have two rulers.

"Oh, look at this one!" Razeq, my older brother, whispered in my ear. He placed his hands in front of the gas lamp to make a shadow animal, which brought me a smile and a feeling of calm. It was the third or the fourth night we'd left our warm mattresses. We hid in the farthest corner of the moldy, dark basement so the bullets that once had opened my brother Naser's chest and wounded him would not find us.

Unlike the last time, Razeq did not cover my ears when gunshots reverberated. By now, some of us had gotten used to the war roaring outside, threatening our lives. I think Razeq was the only one who wasn't scared. He said God's name only when Baba was reading his lips. *Dear God, you are the mighty God who gave life to us, so take it if you wish, but forgive our sins.* Baba said a similar prayer for everyone, even me. I was told that although I was a child of five, the youngest, who had committed no sins, Baba included my name anyway.

Nana, my mother, stopped praying and sat next to me, with Zia, my sister, fastening her arms around both of us. It wasn't cold, but she shivered. I felt a little safer when I was near her but also hungry and sleepy.

As a young child, I could not fully understand the role of seconds, minutes, and hours, but while we were locked in the basement, it felt as if one of the bullets hit the clock and caused it to stop. The little gas lamp, the only light in the darkness, was running out of life. Unlike other nights, we heard no dogs barking and no crickets singing. Even the moon was hidden behind the clouds; fear was everywhere. The last bullets were on their way to hit buildings, birdhouses, humans, children, and even the souls flying in the sky looking for peace. I heard no more gunshots. The hope that had once escaped us found its way into the empty basement again, letting us know that there was a possibility we would still be living tomorrow.

In the morning the next day, I woke up to the sound of Nana's old sewing machine, probably making my dress for Eid. The holiday of Eid, the biggest celebration for Muslims, could bring light to darkness, happiness to sad people, joy to broken hearts, and peace between bloody enemies. On that day, no one could distinguish poor from rich and rich from poor. Everyone was dressed so neatly and treated equally by passersby.

I could hear Latif and Zia walking in the front yard of the house arguing about who would clean and cook. "Why don't you ask Zaher to clean?" Zia asked a question that could never be forgotten, since she repeated it so often. Like always, she was frustrated with Zaher, our youngest brother, who was privileged just because he was a boy.

This was probably the reason why each time Zia saw a shooting star she screamed, "I want to be a boy!"—a sentence that she had learned from Latif, who had learned it from Aziz, my oldest sister. I learned it from Zia. But would I ever wish to be a boy?

"Washing your face with some cold water will help you to wake up," Nana yelled from the other side of the common room. I wanted to sleep more. Everything looked so calm, as if the war that had happened last night was just a nightmare.

Baba knew that leaving the house meant walking alongside the Taliban fighters who had sent bullets our way the night before. He and my brothers were searching for jobs, which were becoming scarce as the war was becoming more intense.

"I need you to try this on for me," Nana said, as she connected pieces of fabric. The excitement of having a new dress encouraged me to leave my bed. The dress was just my size. It fit me better than the one that the famous tailor in our old neighborhood had made for me, which was still too big.

Nana could not read or write, and neither could the rest of us. But her measurements were flawless. She'd known my size by hugging me.

"Beautiful!" I told her. She was happy that I liked the dress so much.

A few days away from Eid we were as excited as if it were already here. The day before the holiday, our tablecloth would be decorated with all kinds of food from the city of Herat: dry and fresh fruits, cookies, roasted nuts, and Nana's homemade bread, *qalef*, which was worth waiting for, even for a year.

Eid was home; my dress was proof of its arrival. I kept looking at myself in the large mirror in Razeq's room. The secret room. Its four walls were covered with long plain curtains, but behind them was a new, colorful world forbidden by the Taliban—and Baba.

Nana knew of the room; I think everyone knew the secret except Baba. There were posters of Bollywood actresses with no hijabs, swans in the shape of a heart, pictures of sunsets with two or more lovers kissing, pictures of nature, pictures of blue seas, and pictures of the Afghan music icon Ahmad Zahir, with his beautiful dark hair. Pictures of practically everything that was banned in Afghanistan.

The Taliban had made it clear that if they found posters not related to Islam, the sinner would be punished and executed in public. There was enough evidence on Razeq's walls to bring an end to his life. This fact had worried Nana, who lectured Razeq about the consequences of disobeying the Taliban's rules. She told him about the importance of listening to the Quran and praying five times a day. Razeq's ears, however, were closed doors.

I was still looking at my reflection in the cracked mirror when I heard someone knocking on the door. I ran, so excited to show my new dress to whoever was there. It was Razeq with his girlfriend, Marjan, whom he loved more than God, as he once said out loud. Baba soon made him pay for the statement. She was about fifteen years old, one year younger than Razeq. Nana believed the age gap was too small, as men usually married women at least three years younger. But Razeq didn't care about any of that; even if Marjan had been older than him, he would have loved her just the same.

Nana never liked it when Marjan visited. She was scared of Marjan's little brother, maybe two years older than me, who sometimes escorted her to our house. This time he was not there. Razeq had probably escorted her.

"Salaam, Marjan," said Latif, kissing her on the cheeks. Marjan looked at me and said, "Kokosto, you look stunning!" She always called me by my nickname, which means laughing dove. "You will see my dress too—the same color!" said Marjan as Razeq guided her into the room.

"Come in!" Razeq made his way back to us in the front yard. He grabbed me by my hands and began to spin me, then let go. I walked around the yard trying to find my balance, the whole yard spinning around me. *Shlup!* I fell to the ground. "Ha-ha!" I could hear him laugh. This was his favorite part of the game. He laughed and laughed, making his way to the well to wash his dusty face and hands with cold, fresh water.

"Did you leave work again?" Nana asked Razeq.

"Shush, Marjan is here, Nana," Razeq whispered, so Marjan wouldn't learn that he was going to be in trouble. He knew that convincing Nana wasn't easy; it took time and energy. He wanted to focus on Marjan.

"You are such a bad influence on your single sisters," Nana said. "If you break the rules, leave work, or lie one more time, I will help your father to break your bones."

"Deal!" said Razeq, knowing that Nana would always have

his back, no matter what. He cleaned his face with her long scarf and swiftly found his way toward the room.

I was surprised that Latif didn't frown on the extra work of making tea for them on top of her assigned duties for the day. I think she loved Marjan, or maybe it's better to say she loved any visitors, since she wasn't allowed to go outside to make friends.

Latif filled the old tea kettle with water and put it on the two shoulders of the fire pit. She added some more wood, put the match under the plastic bag to start the fire, and began to blow the part of the wood that had caught on fire.

"This careless boy is going to put all of us in danger one day," Nana said quietly to herself.

We could hear Razeq and Marjan laugh. I wished I could be in the room with them. Latif probably wished she could experience love too. She was allowed to fall in love only with the characters of Bollywood movies, the people that we called "unreal people."

Once, Aziz asked about Nana's love story. "There was no love," Nana said. "Your Baba built my father a house; in return, your grandfather gave me to your father. I was exchanged for a house." That short sentence ended her story, as if her life had ended when she was sold into marriage.

"But don't hate your grandfather," she continued. "He did what everyone else did—marrying their daughters at a young age to someone they did not know. It did not matter if there was love between them or not because the love will eventually come after marriage." Nana repeated her usual response to questions about love.

I knew Nana was lying to Aziz. She was married to Baba for years, had eight kids, and still did not love or like him. She could barely handle sleeping next to him. Sometimes she would use me as a block to put between herself and Baba.

As I listened, I struggled with the wooden doll—my first—that Latif once taught me to make. "Let me help you," she said. She shortened the stick that was supposed to hold the head, hands, and legs. The doll was a collection of small pieces of fabric from Nana's sewing, meant to show all the characteristics that a homemade doll could have. After Latif's last touch on the doll's hair, I ran to the other room and played. Then I heard Zaher and Latif speaking of Uncle Ghani. There was nothing more fun than going to Uncle's house, eating chocolate, and watching movies on the black and white TV! Those Bollywood movies once inspired Baba to make me the black sheep in the family by naming me Sonita, while all my siblings had names from the Quran.

When we arrived at Uncle Ghani's house, Baba reminded me to kiss Uncle's hand to pay respect to him. He was close to Baba's age but had fewer gray hairs. If I was with Baba and Uncle, people would think that Baba was my grandfather and Uncle was my father.

After we greeted each other, we were guided to the common room on the first floor, where we usually did the weekly gathering. A few minutes passed, and Uncle's older daughter, Latif's close friend, brought tea and chocolate.

It was time to forget the outside world. Uncle and his older son, Hasan, brought down the TV from the roof. Nana; Latif; Khala Zarifa, Uncle Ghani's wife; and her two older daughters began to cover all the windows. The light of the TV was a great risk as it was banned. The moment Uncle turned it on, the women quit gossiping, elders rushed their prayers, boys stopped playing, and I stopped looking for chocolate. We fixed our eyes on the black-and-white screen. Sometimes it made us feel as if we had nothing, but at the same time, we had everything, just to see a different world.

"So handsome!" Latif said about the leading man. Then she lowered her voice; she had to watch what she said. The whole room was silent, allowing the movie to take us under its spell. None of us spoke Hindi, but we followed the story through gestures and facial expressions.

Baba sat with me and Uncle in the first row. Even though he hated to see women with no hijabs, he had to finish the movie just to see the result of all the drama.

"Who were the Taliban fighting last night?" asked Uncle, as if Baba were on the front lines of the battle.

"Probably Ismael Khan's supporters, not sure," Baba said.

"It's a little weird that I don't hear gunshots tonight," said Uncle.

"It's because the Taliban won, and the city is under their control, so why should they waste bullets?"

Then Uncle said to Baba: "The reason that I asked you to bring your family here tonight is that this will be our last gathering, Payandeh. As you noticed, we sold most of our belongings to be able to pay a smuggler to take us to Iran."

"But where will you go?" Baba asked. "At least here you have a place to hide or shelter."

Uncle told my father that they were leaving because they couldn't always hide. "We want to live and breathe freely," he said. "Look at the people on TV; don't you want to live like them? In peace?"

Then he continued: "Iran isn't too far from us. The smuggler will take us there in a few days."

I think everyone in the room could hear them talk. If

someone wanted both of them to shut up, they had to have the courage to ask the elders to keep quiet; therefore, the conversation went on and on until I fell asleep.

I realized the movie was over when I awoke on the back of my older brother Naser, walking on the muddy roads that led back to our house. The stars looked so bright, as if they were just born. The only thing I could hear were the sounds of crickets, footsteps, and the conversation between Baba and Nana. They spoke of Uncle's upcoming journey in guilty voices, as if the Taliban could hear of the plan.

"In the public shower, I heard a lot of stories of people making it to Iran," said Nana to Baba. "It sounds like it is much safer than here." I wasn't sure whether she said that because she was trying to help Baba feel better about the long journey Uncle had ahead of him or because she was telling Baba to follow the same path. If that was Nana's plan, did it mean that we would live like the people we saw in the movies?

2

Ranjita

At the beginning of a new day, I could hear the boys playing outside. I felt lonely, like Baba's God. Hoping for some distraction, I opened the front door of our house, and I saw a little girl seated by the door of the house next to ours. Her mother had been the lady who first told Nana about Iran. She, her husband, and the little girl had lived in Iran before rushing back to Afghanistan to take care of her sick parents.

I liked her mother, but the little girl was hard to understand. I could see why all the boys and girls at the Masjid Safid (White Mosque) laughed at her and didn't seem to like her; she wasn't one of us. She looked too clean, with brushed hair, and no marks of food dripping on her clothing nor dry spots on her skin, something that every winter left on my face and hands. Besides her strange appearance, her funny Iranian accent widened the gap between us. She called her Nana "Mamani" and her Baba "Aqaei."

The day before, I had joined all the kids in laughing at her for annoying our boring religious teacher, the Akhund. He wouldn't let any girls without a scarf into God's house. There were about twenty-five of us in the mosque, mostly boys. Unlike us girls, they had the freedom to be friends with other boys, or even girls.

But girls had to stay away from boys to avoid being punished by the Akhund and their parents.

Each day I failed to find a friend. I had no expectation that that day would be different. I looked down toward the end of our long alley and saw only boys playing marbles. One of the boys I saw was Beshir—though he called himself Shir Khan. I disliked him so much for always excluding me from games just because I was a girl. How could I make friends? Most of the girls in our neighborhood had to stay at home to learn how to cook and clean.

I was about to close the door and go back inside when I saw something unique. I couldn't believe it. The little girl had the doll that I had always wanted to have—with long blond hair, a short dress, and beautiful, long, removable boots. It was her, my dream doll! I had seen her when Nana took me shopping one day, but she thought I didn't deserve the doll since I said bad words right after promising her not to, and I ate too much chocolate when there was any to eat. I didn't brush my hair, I did my chores only when I felt like it, and most important, I protested each time Baba or Nana asked me to go to the mosque to learn the Quran.

I stood by the door and watched the girl closely. I ran inside the house, grabbed the doll that Latif had made, and met her back outside. The dolls could not have been more different. My wooden doll was more like a domestic Afghan woman; hers, more like a foreigner. Like her.

The girl greeted me first. "Salaam. What is the name of your doll?" she asked.

What was the name of my doll? She had no name. I didn't care, because as soon as she married, she would be nameless, like Aziz and Nana. I still didn't know Nana's name. Everyone called her by my oldest brother's name, "Naser's mom," or "the wife of Mullah Payandeh." No one used her name; probably by then, Nana had forgotten her name too.

"What's your doll's name?" I asked her. When my shadow provided some shade, she stopped squinting her eyes and said, "Saara."

Then I asked her, "What is your name?"

"Ranjita."

Oh! Finally, I remembered. Ranjita stood up, and her head came to my shoulder. It was my first time realizing that she was much smaller than me.

"You can play there, and I will play here." She drew an imaginary line on her carpet and invited me to play with her. "What is your name?"

"Sonita," I responded quickly, seeing that she had more toys than I could believe. "Do you want to exchange dolls just to play?" I asked.

I thought she might say no. Mine was a piece of wood. She did have legs, but not like Saara's. She did not have shoes, a purse, golden hair, or most important, white skin, but she had a nice dress that was made from the leftovers of my Eid dress. Latif did such a great job sewing the dress for the doll, but it couldn't come off, so she was stuck with one dress, unlike Saara.

After a few seconds, Ranjita put down my doll and began to dig into her bag to find more toys. I couldn't understand: Nana told me that no kids in Herat had more than two or three toys. I couldn't stop admiring the doll, her beautiful golden hair, so soft and silky, and her beautiful blue eyes. She had boobs too. Hers were better because my doll always needed some adjustment to make them both even. Still figuring out what to play with, Ranjita found more pencil colors—red, blue, yellow, and green, my favorite.

I knew she was more comfortable with the Iranian language, so out of curiosity, I picked a few toys to find out their names in the language that she mostly spoke. "How do you say '*arosak*' in Iran?"

"*Arosak*," she said. I was surprised that they called a doll a doll. I asked her to name the toys on the carpet, and only five or six of them had different names. I thought it was going to be easy to learn Persian, the Iranian language; maybe I could teach her more Hirati, my language.

While I was picking stuff from her toy bag so she could name them for me, I saw a sketchbook. I pointed at the flower and asked, "Did you draw that?"

"No, my Aqaei did that one, but I drew this flower." Hers was not as beautiful as her father's, but it was way better than what I could do.

"How about that one?" I pointed at the other page, which had a drawing of a tall tree, green with apples hanging from it. It looked like the trees in the farms in Shadijan village. That's where we usually went with family to help with the harvest, and in return, our relatives would give us full buckets of Fakhri grapes, pomegranates, sugar apples, and many other types of fruit.

So many beautiful drawings! Suddenly I was less interested in Ranjita's doll and more interested in her; she was full of creativity. It was my first time seeing a child hold a pen to create. "Wow, I have never seen this color before, and that, and these, and those," I said as I pointed. I understood how gray our lives were only when I saw all the colors in front of me.

"Do you know how to draw people?" I asked Ranjita.

"Yes, I do, do you?" I said no—I had never had a pencil to try; plus, it must be hard to draw people.

"Do you want me to draw you?" Ranjita asked me. I said yes instantly—I had never seen a drawing of myself before—not even a photograph.

She found the best spot and directed me to stand there, near the wall. "Don't move, I need to see half of your face," she said. I could see her from the corner of my eye, moving back and forth. I was standing in the middle of the skinny alley, facing the house at the end, where the boys were shouting at each other and complaining about the other team cheating.

"It's done," she said. "Close your eyes." I followed her command, and she took me near the cemetery wall located in front of our houses and told me to open my eyes. I looked at her hands and the ground, expecting to see a piece of paper with my image on it. "Look at the wall," said Ranjita, seeing my confusion. I looked at the wall of their house, and there it was—my profile. My hair was longer, but the rest of the drawing felt right to me. I wished it were on a piece of paper so I could keep it forever.

"Can I try it too?" I asked her. "Will you teach me?"

"Yes, it's very easy. Make me stand where the sun gives you a better image of my profile, and then pick a pen and draw around the lines of the shadow on the wall," said Ranjita.

"Wow, where did you learn that?" I asked.

"I learned it in Mahde Kodak," she said.

"What is a Mahde Kodak?"

"Where children go to learn counting, drawing, and many other things," she said.

Now I knew why she was so different from all of us: she was educated. I was so excited about my first drawing lesson. It was fun, and although I struggled with the hair, I enjoyed the struggle.

"Done!" I said. Ranjita stepped back and I stood next to her. "We're facing each other!" she said, smiling with satisfaction. Then Ranjita put all the colored pencils in front of me and told me to pick one. She gave me the color I picked, green. I couldn't believe it. On top of giving me a big smile, she also gave me a blank piece of paper so I could unleash my imagination.

My friend, Ranjita

I was looking at the pencil and trying to find a way to thank her when Latif interrupted me. She didn't seem happy to see me finding a friend, because she knew from now on, it would be even harder for me to complete my chores on time. I grabbed my doll to leave.

"We can draw flowers tomorrow," said Ranjita, assuring me that we were going to hang out again.

The beginning of the new week meant deep cleaning for everyone—and there was no hot water at home. The only place that would be satisfying to Nana, Latif, and maybe Zia, was the public shower that Ata, Aziz's husband, owned. Aziz was assigned to run it when it was open to women. The public shower would be open to men early in the morning, and after men, it was open to women, who had to be escorted there by a man.

I never understood the point of walking such a long distance to wash only to be covered by dust again on the way home because of the strong winds that blew dirt from the ground into the air. I looked dirtier after coming back from the public shower.

"Move it, my sister, you don't want to miss seeing the women of Herat naked," said Razeq. Baba stopped his morning prayer, looking at Razeq with disappointment. Now he had the image of naked women in his mind while he was imagining himself to be at the Kaaba, God's house, which he and Nana dreamed of visiting one day.

"If you see Marjan, tell her '*dooset daram*' [I love you]," Razeq whispered in my ear, trying not to interrupt Baba's prayers again. Then he whispered the same thing to Latif, thinking that she would be a more reliable person than me to deliver such an important message.

On the way to the shower, we saw a few passersby—farmers rushing to sell their fruits before they started to look bad under the heat of the sun. Then Razeq said saw a car full of Taliban fighters parked in the far distance. "Motherfuckers," he said.

Nana smacked him and said: "You don't believe in God, you don't respect your father's opinion, you curse inside and outside the house. What should I do with you, stupid boy? Your thoughts and language can kill you and me. For once, be like one of us; stop questioning and obey if you want to stay alive."

"That is actually leading us to a good point," Razeq said. "I don't want to be one of you. I don't want to live in fear anymore, Nana!" I felt sadness in my brother's words. Nana no longer argued. She slowed down, and once again, Razeq and I were ahead of everyone.

"Kokosto, don't let Nana, Baba, or the Taliban motherfuckers tell you how to think," he mumbled. "And don't let them stop you from cursing. It makes you feel free. If you ever encounter a bully, tell them 'Fuck your mother.'"

"Fuck your mother," I repeated, so I could remember to tell that to the bully of our alley, Shir Khan.

When we arrived at the public shower, Razeq left. "Salaam, Nana," Aziz greeted us. "How are you all doing? How is Baba?" Her face was not the way I remembered. Nana kissed Aziz on her left cheek, which had fewer bruises, and said nothing, as if she knew the story.

But Latif asked, "Who did that to you this time?" Instead of answering, Aziz gave us lollipops and changed the conversation. It wasn't too hard to guess who did it. It was probably Amid again, Aziz's brother-in-law, who often caused Aziz pain. Ata had given Amid permission to beat Aziz if she misbehaved. For Amid, Aziz was a punching bag that had to endure his anger.

I had seen Amid beating Aziz a few months earlier. I don't remember the reason why he was screaming, but I clearly remember him dropping his bike on Aziz's head. She didn't cry, since her voice was just another form of misbehavior.

I had realized how deeply she was wounded when her blood dripped on the ground of our house. Nana did everything to stop it but failed. Aziz hadn't slept that night and kept us all awake. She walked back and forth as Nana and Latif held her arm. She cried from pain, or maybe something else that I didn't understand. She kept walking and walking until something dropped from between her legs.

In the morning, when I woke up, she was asleep and several blankets covered her. Nana gave me a black plastic bag to bury somewhere in the cemetery in front of our house. The bag smelled like blood. I took it and left the house. My curious mind stole my patience, and soon I found a place in the cemetery where I could sit down and see what was in the bag. My small and weak hands failed to open the knots, so I ripped the bag open, and suddenly the blood found its way onto the dusty ground. In the bag were big pieces of meat, and between them was a human baby. The baby's eyes were closed, the head was so small, the fingers were not separated yet.

I felt sick, like throwing up from the smell and what I had found in the bag. Soon the smell of blood attracted three or four homeless dogs. They ran so fast toward me that I had just a few seconds to make a smart move before they attacked me. I ran toward the wall that was near our house, forgetting about the baby. There was no need for me to jump: the dogs stopped at the plastic bag and ate Aziz's baby.

I felt a mix of everything—fear, disgust, sadness. I couldn't look at the dogs, licking the ground with blood around their mouths. I ran to the Karbar, the river near our house, and sat in the shallow part of it, waiting for the disgust to leave my body.

Now, here at the shower, Aziz gave me another lollipop. I had missed seeing her. Unlike Latif, she was always okay with me making a mess, getting into trouble, and going to the Karbar. Zia and I always enjoyed being assigned to go to Aziz's house to take care of her baby daughter, Nasim, while Ata was busy at work or at the gambling parties organized by his brother Amid.

Although Aziz wasn't Amid's wife, she had to do whatever he asked. Usually, she had to cook and clean nonstop. Running the shower was probably her favorite job.

Like Nana, Aziz had also married young. I'm not sure at what age since we don't have a record of ages in my family, but Nana thinks it was the winter when I was born. Aziz thinks she was probably fourteen when she married—two years older than Nana had been. Nana was so young when she married that she didn't understand her relation to Baba. She called him Uncle for a long time, until someone helped her understand that Baba was her husband, not her uncle.

"Let's go before the water gets cold." Latif and I led the way. I liked going to the shower, not to wash, but to find girls my age to play with.

"Oh, it's our neighbor," Latif said, walking toward a lady sitting down with a girl my age. Ranjita! I began to walk faster. "Salaam, Khala Afsalneh," Latif said to Ranjita's mother. I wasn't surprised that Latif called her Aunt, because she was friendly with everyone and made them feel like a family member. Soon Nana and Zia joined us. Nana put the bucket down to fill it with water and began to speak with Ranjita's mother.

She had skin as white as snow—something that every girl wished to have in Afghanistan. And she had big breasts, which Zia and I wished to have. Next to Ranjita's mother, Nana appeared to be an old woman with breasts that were like two deflated balloons.

Ranjita and I began to chase each other in the shower, even though it was dangerous to run on the slippery floor. "Sit down, you two, before you break your heads," screamed one of the ladies from the other side of the shower. We went inside one of the smaller stalls, covering ourselves with suds from too much shampoo. It was so much fun, not being able to see through the suds and searching for the pool of water in which to rinse them off.

Soon Ranjita left, and we got ready to leave too. Latif helped me to put on my dress and pants. I went outside to meet Razeq. "Kiss Baba's hand for me," Aziz said. "I'll see you all soon!"

As we were walking home, I saw kids with the Siparah and the Quran all rushing in one direction. "I heard you are going to the mosque again to learn Siparah," Razeq said to me while watching the children going to the mosque. "I'm not going back," I told him angrily, not being happy about what Nana and Baba had planned for my day. The same thing!

The difference between the public shower and the mosque was that the mosque was painted white, as opposed to the shower's dark brown. Through a window, the light of the sun could shine to help the children see their lessons. But sometimes we didn't need the light because we had to memorize our lessons, so we could recite them with our eyes open or closed.

On my first day at the mosque, the Akhund beat three or four children who couldn't read their lessons properly. The day after, I was next, so I started to hate learning. I hated the Akhund too, and his stick that always made one of us cry.

"What does the stupid Akhund teach you that the streets can't?" Razeq asked. "For him, you are just a mynah bird that can learn to speak, not to think. 'Aleph, Beh, now repeat after me'—isn't this what he teaches you? He fills your head with useless lessons and beliefs so you won't have room to learn useful stuff." I was happy that Nana was walking in front of us and couldn't hear.

Nana put a scarf on my head, gave me the Siparah to go to the mosque, and disappeared with the rest into our alley. A few kids entered the mosque while I stood by the door, thinking about which direction to go. All the excitement was happening on the other side of the Karbar, so close, and yet it seemed impossible to cross the water. Still, the other side of the Karbar was looking fresh, green. I took my first step into the cold water. With the second step and third, the cold ran throughout my body. I could see the little rocks on the bottom of the river. It was time for her, the river, to relax.

Greenland, the name I gave to the other side of the river, was so close. I took more steps; the pureness of the water turned blurry, and I could no longer see my feet. The water climbed up my body as I moved forward. Moving took more and more energy. I was cold and scared, but I decided to take another step forward. I lifted up my foot and brought it down to land in the same depth of water, but my foot couldn't find the body of the river to touch. Agitated, afraid, and alone, I was pushed into the deeper part of the river.

I felt as if the hole on the river's surface was a mouth, opened up to swallow me. I was struggling to keep my mouth and nose above the water; I tried and tried. I surprised the river with the desire I had for living, and the river surprised me with the amount of fight it put against my will. My shoes were long gone; I could feel that the river was winning.

I was letting my hands and feet relax when my feet hit the ground. The moment my head was above water, I began to cough so much that my ears and eyes hurt. I couldn't breathe, even though I was on the surface with the air around me. I don't recall if anyone was there to ask for help. I just dragged my body onto the sand and waited to catch my breath, thinking,

What will Nana say about losing my shoes? What will Latif say about looking dirty again?

Once I could walk, I headed home. When I opened the entrance door, Latif stared at me in disbelief. "You were much cleaner before going to the shower this morning," she said. "I'm gonna kill you and bury you by that sewage river!" Latif went on and on, not knowing that the river already had tried to kill me. She always wanted me to look good and presentable on the outside, not knowing that inside I felt scared and bad.

That day I learned that we never looked into each other's eyes to see the fear or happiness present in them. We never asked each other, "How are you feeling?" Latif tried so hard to keep me looking clean on the outside because neighbors judged each other by what they wore and how they looked, and never knew how they felt inside.

Nana often came up with various kidnapping stories to prevent me from leaving the house. But now she wanted me to go outside and play instead of teaching Latif and Zia how to draw flowers, which was distracting them from their duties. With the leftovers of the green pencil, Zia had drawn a house with big windows. I was sure she could have turned it into something so beautiful if the green pencil could have lasted just a few more minutes.

In the afternoon, my favorite time of day, I was asked to sprinkle water all around the dusty yard. A big carpet in the middle of a clean, cool yard; black and green tea with *shirpara*, my favorite Afghan sweet; and family members—this was the recipe for a happy afternoon. That day was going to be even more special once Aziz and her family arrived.

"Salaam, Nana, *muah, muah*!" Aziz said as she kissed us. She seemed happier, and I thought she had done such a nice job covering her bruises with makeup.

"Pour me some tea!" Ata demanded, as he found his comfortable spot around the large carpet, took out some cards, and prepared the game.

"You still carry cards with you?" asked Baba with concern and disappointment, knowing that Ata usually gambled with them.

"Kaka, my uncle, I only use them for fun. There will be no money involved tonight, but if Naser wants to bet you, that would be a different story." Ata's joke put a crack on Baba's lips. Ata and Baba could be good friends if Baba would stop bringing religion into every conversation, and if Ata could accept everything Baba said about religion—which was almost impossible.

"Kaka, if you wanted a mullah in your family, why did you agree to give me Aziz?" Ata ended his question with a smirk.

"Well, I thought that God might guide you on the right path," Baba said.

"And I am telling you that this path that I am on is the right path because it keeps me happy. Will you join me?" Ata shuffled the cards and smiled with Razeq, who was more in favor of following Ata's path than Baba's.

This is how Baba and Ata welcomed each other, with a conversation that would do no good for either of them. "I swear, life would be so much better without men," Aziz said, then quickly added, "not you, Baba, you are an angel." She rushed to finish her tea when she heard that Faize, Baba's nephew, was going to join us that night.

Aziz and Razeq ran to the common room with a gas lamp,

looking for something. "They're going to play a prank on Faize," said Latif, helping them put on black dresses. In just a few seconds, Aziz and Razeq looked like Talibs, with long black dresses and black eyeliner.

"Come on, Razeq, find something black to put around your head! Latif, don't open the door to Faize until you have our signal," said Aziz. Nana was laughing, and soon Baba joined us in the living room, looking entertained. "How do I look?" Aziz asked.

Razeq responded jokingly, "Uglier than before, my sister."

Baba was impressed by how quickly Aziz managed to change her appearance. She even took off her scarf and put a turban around her head. Her eyes were looking messy, as if Atiq, her baby boy, had done her makeup.

"No one should come outside; you can watch from the window," Aziz said, as she and Razeq made their way to the yard. Then we heard steps approaching our door.

Knock! Knock! Finally, Faize was there!

Aziz gave Razeq the signal. The night was even darker now, so Faize could not easily see Aziz's or Razeq's faces. "Come inside," Razeq said to Faize, without saying anything to greet him. Razeq sounded serious.

The moment Faize put his foot inside the door, Razeq pushed him against the wall and said in a deeper voice, "We were waiting for you!"

Suddenly Faize put his hands up and appeared to be scared, but he said nothing, as if he were waiting to hear the voice once again. "Face the wall," Aziz told Faize and closed the door. I could hear the giggles of everyone from the living room.

Aziz took playing cards out of Faize's pocket, handed them to Razeq, and demanded, "What else do you have in your pockets?"

"I'm just here to visit relatives," Faize said, thinking that no matter what the reason for the visit was, he was going to meet his punishment since he was carrying cards around. Aziz took something else out of Faize's pocket, looked at it, and then said, "Did you know that snuff tobacco powders are made of chicken poop?"

This made Razeq laugh, so he quietly left the scene. Faize looked suspicious, even putting down his hands, but he still faced the wall. Aziz was still talking as if nothing suspicious had happened.

"Don't turn your head!" she ordered Faize, who was now aware of the game. But Aziz thought that the game was still going on.

"Are my relatives arrested?" asked Faize. But then suddenly he yelled—YOW! I'm not sure what Aziz's reaction was, but I jumped in my place. Faize turned and hit under Aziz's turban, laughing, "Ha-ha, you scared me!"

Now the game was over, and Faize could pull himself together. "You think that snuff powder is made of chicken poop?" he asked Aziz as he made his way toward the carpet where the rest of the audience had gathered.

Baba greeted Faize and gave him a cup of tea. "Were you involved in this game, Kaka?" Faize asked Baba.

"He wrote the whole script!" Naser joked. Everyone laughed.

3

Love and Forced Marriage

"I need your help with building the fire, Sonita," said Latif the next morning. I was shocked and honored that she thought I could be a good accomplice for such a big mission. To accomplish such a goal I needed to confront my fear of going to the basement to fetch wood.

It didn't matter if it was nighttime or daytime. In the basement—where we went whenever speeding bullets made the surface unsafe—it was always nighttime.

I was scared of the unknown hidden in the darkness. Almost all of the scary stories told by Bibi, Aziz's mother-in-law, ended up in the dark basement where she said jinns, invisible creatures, lived. At the end of each horror story, she would demand that we change our bad behaviors. If we didn't, the jinns would haunt us. I had not changed any of my bad behaviors, so I feared they would show themselves to me.

As I took my first step down the stairs, I felt my courage fading away. The moment I passed the fifth or sixth stair, I ran back upstairs.

"Never mind, I'll do it," said Latif and continued sweeping the yard. There it was, the moment I got fired without even starting my job.

But I was curious to know what would happen if I faced my fear. So I stood at the top of the stairs leading down to the basement. I told myself, *Latif does this all the time, so I can do it too!* Courage slowly made its way back to me. I set a goal for myself: going down there and facing my fear. My legs took me down to the basement. Then I ran to the middle of the room, grabbed two or three pieces of wood, and ran back toward the light. I made it and I felt like a hero.

Latif threw a box of matches near my foot; another chance to try my ability. I lit the fire, and once it reached the center of the wood, I put the big smoky pot on the shoulder of the fire pit and put some water in it.

It was the first time that I realized how dark and smoky the kitchen was—and the first time I realized how difficult Latif's job was. She had to go into the basement every day alone, and then struggle with the wood, not wanting to be burned as she lit the fire. She cried each time the smoke found its way into her eyes.

If someone were to challenge me and Latif to name a few colors, I think she would probably lose because her view of colors was dominated by the gray, white, and black of smoky kitchens. I wished I could take her quickly to the Karbar, where wild purple flowers stood up tall; where I could see my favorite color, green, on the other side where Greenland was; and where the blue water was the most noticeable color before the boys of our neighborhood were unleashed.

I was still in search of oil to put in the pot when I heard Latif laughing out loud. She was laughing at me, but I couldn't tell why. "Come on, Nana has to see you! Nana, I found this child in our house, do you know her?" said Latif. Nana joined Latif, and they both laughed.

Latif grabbed a broken mirror. "Who do you see in the mirror?" she asked. I looked in the mirror, and the only parts of my face that the smoke had not touched were my eyes and teeth.

"Take her outside and wash her by the well before she touches anything," Nana said, giving Latif a new assignment—to clean me again!

"Come here before I chase you all around the house," said Latif, laughing. I wasn't sure what joy Latif found in wanting to wash me. "Stop touching everything," she said, as I looked for a way to escape her.

I ran to the other side of the yard, toward the well but realized that both Latif and Zia were joyfully blocking my way. They grabbed me. "Hold her! Hold her!" Splash! Suddenly I felt like I was in a big bucket of ice water.

Once I escaped them I sat near the door, close to the warmth of the heated walls. I heard the cry of the man who sells the Afghan ice cream called *shiryakh*. When the seller saw me, a child, he changed the direction of his small vending cart and started to come toward our alley. He stopped a few steps away from our door, in the middle of the alley, and yelled, "I have delicious *shiryakh*, come before it's gone!" He was in a rush, since the day was still hot. Soon a few children came out of their houses.

The *shiryakh* seller, who was skinny and tall, grabbed the wrinkled money from the children, licked his thumb, and began to count.

"Nana!" I yelled. I couldn't bear the presence of *shiryakh* and not eat it. I stood near the door and put aside the curtain, meant to prevent strangers from seeing the women inside the house. "Nana!" I yelled again.

Suddenly Latif appeared from the other side of the curtain and grabbed me by my hand. "I got you!" It was once again time for me to kick and grab whatever could stop me from being taken back to the icy water by Latif. I was between the entrance door and outside, but Latif wasn't making any attempts to force me inside the yard. She let go of me, and I ran outside, where she was not allowed to be without a male. I ran toward the main road and stood where I thought I was safe—and learned why Latif suddenly lost her interest in taking me inside.

The *shiryakh* guy, looking nervous, took off his hat and brushed his black hair back with his fingers. His focus had shifted from making money to Latif, who was standing by the door like a statue, looking at him.

Finally, he decided to cut the uncomfortable eye contact and put a spoon in the big pot where the *shiryakh* was kept cool. He grabbed a bowl and put a big scoop of *shiryakh* in it. Then he put the best topping on it, which none of the kids ever got—pistachio. And he gave it to Latif.

She took the bowl from him so delicately, as if it were a rose, like in the Bollywood movies. In just this short encounter, Latif felt as if she knew him from her dreams and could trust him with her life.

Then she realized that she had no hijab and was in the presence of a stranger. Latif already had been struggling with a lack of suitors, and if people saw her standing by the door without a hijab, no one would want to marry her. So she left.

The moment she was gone, the *shiryakh* guy also left. But he seemed much happier than when he had entered our alley.

"Why are you so happy, Latif?" Nana asked. I was dying to answer Nana's question, but I didn't want Latif to be killed for falling in love with a real person, rather than just the characters in Bollywood movies. So I kept quiet. To make the situation seem less suspicious, Latif stopped smiling. But her eyes were full of happiness.

After the day that Latif and the *shiryakh* guy met, he appeared in our neighborhood often. He yelled even louder than before, not to grab children's attention, but to let Latif know that he was there. Sometimes I saw her sneaking out. Sometimes he would give me even more *shiryakh* to go find Latif and let her know he was there. Because of their love, my life was turning upside down—free *shiryakh* in our alley every other hot afternoon!

One day he stayed longer in the alley because Latif didn't rush to leave. She was fearful, but she stayed by the door longer than usual.

Suddenly, Aziz's husband, Ata, entered the alley and saw Latif speaking with a stranger. She closed the door quickly, but it was too late—Ata saw them. He lost control and began to scream every bad word that Razeq had ever taught me. He tried to slap the *shiryakh* guy and threw all his bowls on the ground, ordering him to leave.

I was shocked and afraid to see Ata's anger. I feared for both myself and Latif. She opened the door, maybe to try to beg him not to tell anyone, but as soon as she did, Ata slapped her. He then went in the basement and brought up a piece of wood, which he used to beat her so hard that her screams echoed in my ears. I cried as I watched; I couldn't help her. I wished Nana or Baba were there, but they probably would have beaten Latif too.

Ata kept yelling the word "Shame!" at her. From the corner of the common room, Latif looked at me, holding one side of her face and crying quietly. I knew Ata had beaten her on behalf of Baba, Nana, my brothers, and whoever hated girls who fall in love before marriage. I felt such a strong hatred for him; I wished I could hit him with the same piece of wood. I wished he were dead.

Ata didn't leave the house until Nana, Baba, and everyone arrived home. He immediately reported Latif's behavior as he pointed at her and yelled "Shame!" again. Baba and Nana looked at her with so much disappointment. Latif was probably expecting to be beaten again, but no one touched her. Nana asked her how she could bring shame to them. Latif mostly remained silent because what she had done, fallen in love, was unforgivable.

As days went by, Latif's pain appeared on her forehead in purple and yellow colors. Nana understood the extent of her injuries only when we went to the public shower. Aziz knew how much pain Latif was in as she often had similar bruises.

Slowly Baba, Nana, and my brothers changed their unkind behavior toward Latif. But she had no interest in afternoon teatime, watching Bollywood movies, and the weekly trip to the public shower.

Latif thought that she would never see the *shiryakh* guy again, but one day he came to our house—with his family. Our brother Khaleq opened the door and then rushed to the common room to let Baba and Nana know that we had visitors—or maybe a suitor. When Latif heard that, she ran around making the common room look presentable, even though her face was still messy with small, bruised spots.

Once a curtain was established between the common room and the guest room to keep the men and women separated, Baba welcomed the *shiryakh* guy and his father. Nana stood in the doorway and welcomed the lady under the burqa—his mother; they gave each other kisses on the cheeks. Latif kissed the *shiryakh* guy's mother's hand and took her burqa to hang. The lady handed flowers and sweets in a box to Latif.

Latif had cleaned the glasses, which looked as new as the first day Nana had bought them. After making sure the tea looked and tasted right, Razeq made his way back to the guest room with tea to serve. Like Latif, my brothers were glad to take the day off and meet Latif's lover. I was grateful that Ata wasn't there; otherwise, he would have broken the guy's legs.

I used the opportunity to eat chocolate as the adults got busy talking to each other. Once I got bored of the women's conversation, I went to the room filled with men talking about Latif's future. Only two were engaged in conversation—Baba and the father of the *shiryakh* guy were talking about the war. This always worked miraculously to break the ice, since everyone had something to say about it. Once the men wrapped up the conversation about war, they began to talk about the reason why they had come to our house, which was to ask for Latif's hand in marriage.

"Is your son already married?" Baba asked.

"No, he is not."

"What is his occupation?"

"My son is a *shiryakh foroosh* [ice cream seller]." Nana looked disappointed. Baba often told Razeq that if he didn't learn construction, he might have no choice but to become a *shiryakh* seller. To Baba this was a bad job to have because in the winter no one wanted the cold treat. I guess to Latif it didn't matter what her lover's job was, but to Nana and Baba it meant that he might not be able to pay Latif's cost. When the conversation turned to price, Latif stopped smiling.

Latif was so distracted by the conversation that she didn't pinch me for eating the sweets that were for the guests. The room was so quiet, with everyone listening carefully to the conversation taking place in the guest room where the men were gathered. Everyone was so distracted, it was a good time to leave the house to explore Herat, but I wanted to be there to eat sweets and to hear the bitter conversations that made Latif stop smiling once the subject got to her price.

"How much is *pishkash* [the dowry]?" the father of the *shiryakh* guy asked Baba. While they were bargaining on Latif's price, she stared at the carpet. The guest room was loud, and the women sat quietly.

Latif did a good job of hiding her sadness when the *shiryakh* guy's father said, "We don't possess such money to offer you." He offered another price, but Baba rejected it.

"The *pishkash* still remains the same," Baba said. "You can come back to our house once you have enough financial support to accept the *pishkash*."

As soon as the *shiryakh* guy and his parents left the house, Latif locked herself in the kitchen, where no one could hear her cry.

It took Latif several days to feel a little free of her disappointment and pain. A lack of friends made it more complicated for her to share how she felt, but whenever Aziz paid us a visit or when we had to go to the public shower, Latif opened up to her. Unlike everyone else in my family, Aziz had been okay with Latif's love interest. She even gave Latif hope that the *shiryakh* guy might return in the near future, once he had enough money.

With the help of Aziz, Latif slowly became more herself and started to talk more often. By the time we dressed for a wedding we had been invited to, she was back to normal.

"What if I wear this red shirt with the black maxi skirt?" Latif asked, wanting Baba's and Nana's approval. Nana showed disagreement since the slit of the skirt was a little too high. But Latif didn't give up. She began to put on her favorite outfits. But Nana always disagreed: "No, too big, no, too tight, no, too dark, no, too light." Latif was trying and trying. She changed several outfits but all with the same scarf, as if it was glued to her head. Even though all her body parts were covered, the obstacles from Nana were endless. I couldn't wait for Latif to choose her look so I could decide what to wear to the wedding, which was happening the next day.

"That's better!" Nana finally liked her look even though the skirt was the same one that Latif had tried on first, but now it was with a different shirt. I think Nana just gave up.

Now it was my turn! I ran to the common room toward the wall niche where big and small bundles of clothing were smushed into a bag. Each of us had one; only Latif knew which belonged to whom.

"Here you go, take that to Nana," said Latif, but I opened it right there. If I had let Latif or Nana choose for me, they probably would have picked a dark color so my selection would not make the laundry harder for Latif. I looked at the clothing and chose my favorite blue dress. Unlike Latif, I didn't receive any rejection. For Latif, it was harder since she was older than fifteen and had to behave like a lady so she could find a suitor.

After I drank the first half of my black cardamom tea, I lay on the corner of the carpet and took off my shirt to allow the gentle breeze to cool me. I faced the sky, where I had left millions of stars uncounted.

I was about to break my record counting stars when I heard someone knocking impatiently at the door. As I was always the most curious person in the family, I jumped up and opened it. It was Ali. I never quite understood his relation to me, but Nana said he was her brother-in-law's brother. "My mother sent you this," said Ali, holding a letter in his hands.

"Who is it? Come in!" said Nana. He slowly made his way through the house, but he wouldn't give me the letter. I even reached for it.

"Salaam, Khala," said Ali after giving Nana the card. Right after him, Baba and my brothers entered the yard. Nana welcomed Ali in the chaos, and right after giving Nana the invitation card, he left and refused to eat any *shirpara*.

Latif, Zia, and the boys were also impatient to know where we were invited. Would it be possible to be invited to another wedding? If so, as Nana sometimes described her happiness, it would be an endless joy!

Once Latif was done pouring everyone a cup of tea, she and Zia began to argue about who should first open the card. This was always so much fun—discovering whether an invitation card was for a funeral or a wedding. Baba never took part in this game, so he sat alongside and began to roll his *tasbih* (a cord with ninety-nine beads, symbolizing the ninety-nine names of Allah). Laughing at their struggle, Nana finally decided to give the card to Latif.

"*Khodaya, lotfan, lotfan* [God, please, please]!" Latif begged God to have it be what she wanted to see. Not only her, but we all also hoped for a wedding party.

"If you can't open it, I'll do it!" said Razeq, whose patience was long gone.

Latif looked again at the back of the white envelope, which probably said, "To the Family of Mullah Payandeh." Who knew? Latif slowly took out the card from the envelope. Yay! It was a wedding party! To prove it, Latif showed the card to everyone: there was a picture of a bride and a groom, which meant that it was a wedding invitation. If it was for a funeral, there would be a picture of the moon or stars with God's house.

"This will be Marjan and me soon!" said Razeq after looking at the bride and groom on the front of the card. Baba, who was against Razeq's love story, looked at him with disappointment, mumbled some words, and continued rolling his *tasbih*.

Then, since no one in the family could read, Nana assigned Naser to find out the important information on the card: "Take the card to the mayor of the city to read it; remember where the location is and what time we should be there." It was not surprising that Razeq decided to do Naser's task, since he couldn't wait another minute to learn the time and place of the wedding. We were all missing dancing and hearing music.

When everyone had calmed down, I put my head on Nana's lap. She put her hand on my head and ran her fingers through my hair. I could never get tired of that. I needed it at least once a day, or I would miss Nana, her smell and her touch.

"It's probably Khalil's wedding," Baba said, sharing his guess with the rest of us.

Soon Nana's touch put me to sleep. I could hear, I could feel, but I could not move a muscle. I was so drowned in love, comfort, and happiness. I felt so safe whenever I was close to Nana.

The next morning, we all pushed ourselves into a van that could barely fit ten people and our luggage. We were going to the wedding! After agreeing on the price, the driver closed the door and took us out of the city. The car passed by the big towns in Herat Province, small villages, and short and tall mountains, but there was still no sign of the final destination, as if the driver were lost. After a long time, Zia and I were so thrilled to see the driver making a right turn onto a dusty road that had a few houses.

When he stopped, I got out; the wind moved through my hair, the fresh air felt like the weather of the village of Shadijan. The tall green trees alongside the road not only provided the most pleasant shade but also prevented the wind from blowing the dust around that had settled on the street.

"Salaam, Kaka, welcome everyone!" said Abdul, Nana's brother-in-law, when he saw us entering his house. The four long walls went as far as my eyes could see, standing up tall as if there were a treasure in the house that needed to be protected. The house was divided into two properties that were facing each other, and in the middle of the yard was a pond, probably for the cows and sheep that were at the end of the yard.

Razeq complimented Abdul on the music he was playing. "Wow, beautiful voice," he said. "Who is he?" Abdul was happy to hear Razeq's approval, since he thought that Razeq had the most beautiful voice.

Aunt Nasrin hugged Nana. "Oh my dear God, so happy to see you, Sister." Her made-up face looked like snow; her neck looked brown. Aunt Nasrin often would let Latif, Zia, or even me dip into her paints and powders. Like always, she put a little makeup on Nana.

"Don't make me look like a fourteen-year-old," said Nana.

This was often Nana's concern. I don't know why she was afraid to look younger than her age. While Aunt Nasrin was busy putting makeup on Nana, Latif, Zia, and I took our turns.

"Sonita, that's too bright!" Latif laughed.

"You look like a bride," Nana said to me as she was helping me dress. "I might be able to marry you off sooner than these two! Ha-ha!" Then she told Latif to wear her white scarf. "It makes you look like an adult," she said. Nana wanted to dress her up the way she liked, the way she knew.

Then we made our way to the big hall and found a spot in the corner. A lot of people were there—more children than adults. In the other corner of the room were two girls Latif's age. One was singing and the other one was playing a small drum. She had such a nice voice and energy that most of the kids soon were jumping up and down feeling the energy of the performance.

The bride was seated in the middle of the hall wearing a bright white wedding dress and a shiny silver crown on her head (which didn't match her gold earrings and necklace). All the eyes in the room were on her, and her eyes were on the ground. In front of the bride was a big, delicious cake with bride and groom dolls on the top. Next was a stand mirror for her to look at the groom.

This was my least favorite part: everyone had to wait until the bride and groom looked at each other before they'd cut the cake and then pass pieces to the adults and their hungry kids. I was so excited about the cake and for the bride to put her veil up so I could see her. I wished to be her. She had the most beautiful dress, makeup, and hairstyle—something that Nana said we could have too, but only on our wedding day. I couldn't wait!

Soon Aunt Nasrin entered the hall with the groom, who

was Khaleq's age—maybe fifteen. The moment he sat next to the bride, all eyes shifted to him. Now he was staring at the carpet too. Maybe now the bride could breathe; the room was not staring at her.

Now it was Nana and Aunt Nasrin's turn to show off, singing, "*Allah mubarak kona, Khoda mubarak kona* . . . [God bless you . . .]." The village where the wedding took place was far away from the city, so the Taliban couldn't hear the music. I thought the two girls had done a better job singing, but to be fair, Nana did a better job playing the drum. I was jumping up and down with the other kids when I heard a sad cry mixed with Nana's voice. It was the bride.

Now that her veil was up, I recognized her. We had been at her wedding just a few months before. Why was she marrying again? I was too young to understand what scared her so much that the spoonful of cake in her hand trembled: after her husband had died, she had to marry her brother-in-law.

Still, I was so happy; I danced and clapped and jumped up and down, not knowing that just because it was a wedding didn't mean that everyone would be happy. Probably that day the bride wished to die before she had to sleep with her brother-in-law. Nana continued to sing, despite knowing that this wedding was the funeral of the bride.

No one said anything. Even the groom was silent. He looked so weak, knowing that with tradition against both of them, they had to be wife and husband, they had to sleep together, and they had to have babies.

The next day I didn't see the bride, but I found Baba talking to Uncle Abdul where we had danced the night before. "How much is your final price, Abdul?" Baba asked him. "If we had enough money to get us to Iran, I would never sell our house. I built it with my own hands." Abdul seemed to be happy to have a house in the city where he could stay whenever he needed to sell fruit or animals there.

Someone gave Nana two big bags of cake to eat on the way home and another to give to Aziz. Baba shook Abdul's hand and got in the car. He looked happy. "He will come to the city in a few days to visit us and the house. He is keen to buy the house from us," Baba said to Nana, who soon after put her hands up, mumbling words from the Quran in appreciation. Razeq was so happy that we were preparing to leave for Iran as soon as we sold the house.

"Can we take Aziz, Atiq, and Nasim too?" I asked Nana, who responded to my question positively. I felt better that Aziz was going to be far away from everyone in that house who made her cry.

4

A New Kind of Monster

Sonita, you don't want to be late again," said Nana. I preferred to be late, rather than arriving on time and listening to the Akhund say, "You are going to be punished because of *blah-blah-blah* and *blah-blah-blah*!" This was his remark at the beginning and the end of his teaching. I disliked him, but I could never say that out loud. He was considered to be someone closer to God than any of us just because he could read the whole Quran.

I put some jam inside my bread to eat at the mosque and entered the yard to see Ranjita being questioned by Latif and Zia. They were so surprised that I had made a friend who was clean, polite, smart, and, most important, able to answer questions without irrelevant answers, as I did.

"Can you teach Sonita to be clean and free of lice?" Zia asked. She and Latif laughed. Ha-ha-ha! They laughed again as they looked at me. "Go find your way before the Akhund finds you," said Latif and closed the door after us.

When I knew that Latif or Zia couldn't chase me, I yelled at them, "Big noses!" It felt good!

Ranjita and I walked the empty alley without seeing any of the boys playing. "I think we are the only ones who are late,"

I told Ranjita, suggesting that we escape going to the mosque again. Yesterday, she'd objected: "What if someone is going to steal my slippers again?"

"This time we won't leave anything on the sand," I told her before fear could change her mind. "Look, there are so many boys at the Karbar; it's not just you and me," said Ranjita. The boys were always our greatest fear and the reason why we couldn't play in the alley.

"So what? This river doesn't belong just to them," I said. The truth was that I was scared too, even if my feet were still taking me in their direction.

Soon Ranjita and I found a spot and sat against the tall white walls that marked the mosque's property. I was more scared of the boys in our neighborhood than the homeless dogs that were everywhere. "If the boys try to harm us, we can throw rocks at them and run away," I advised Ranjita. Still, when I tried to hit something with rocks, the rocks only hit the innocent ground. But when the boys aimed rocks at me, one part of my body would always bleed or swell in pain.

Ranjita and I were the only girls, except for one who was with her brother. None of the boys could say a word to her or exclude her from the games. Soon I recognized Shir Khan and a few other boys. Shir was busy chasing his friends in the shallow part of the river. Some boys were lying on the warm sand in the sun, and some of them were standing in line on top of a tall rock practicing how to perfect the frog jump into the water.

"Let's go fishing!" I told Ranjita. I took the scarf off my head, we tightened our slippers around our waists, and we started to walk in the shallow part of the river, where there was a small chance of catching fish by holding a scarf between us.

"One, two, three!" We tried it for the fourth or fifth time. Failed again! Every attempt failed but brought us joy and laughter.

I'm not sure how long we were in the water chasing each other. The big and small fish also liked our games, which would create waves for them and swing them around. To our surprise, soon we caught a big fish!

This was our biggest achievement. We could open its stomach and fry it, but we had no oil or matches, or we could take it home and release it in the well. I heard from one of the boys that fish ate dirt. I thought it could eat all the dirt in our well, so we could have clean water.

"I see why you aren't at the mosque!" I heard the Akhund yelling. Ranjita and I quit fishing, ran toward the wall, and put our wet scarf on us to cover our faces. "Ali, Ahmad, Beshir, Reza . . ." The Akhund listed the names of the boys he saw swimming. I could hear the boys running, calling each other's names, and reminding each other—Ali, your shoes! Ahmad, your shirt! Reza, your Siparah!

Ranjita and I had the safest spot, under the scarf, still laughing at the boys and our cleverness. In just a minute, all the boys vanished—now the river was ours.

We were still enjoying the sun, getting ready to continue fishing, when I heard "Attention! Attention!" An alarming voice was coming from a black Toyota that wasn't too far from us. "Attention!" I can't remember the words that followed, but something being dragged behind the car caught my attention. I stood up; I was still unable to see it. But the figures of the Taliban with guns were clear to me.

"Come with me!" I told Ranjita and ran toward the road the car was on. I ran alongside the car like many others from our neighborhood. The car moved slowly, to give the public time to catch up with it. I continued running in the middle of the street, where now I could see what was being dragged behind the car: two motionless bodies.

Two men were being dragged behind the car. I could see them; I could see their shirtless bodies. Not knowing why, I began to run even faster than some of the adults, who were also chasing the car. My eyes were locked on the bodies, which were as white as the mosque's walls. I could hear the sounds of people running behind and in front of me. Then the black Toyota that was carrying a few Talibs in the back stopped.

I was in the middle of the crowd, struggling to see what was happening. I pushed myself between the adults so I could see better. There I was, standing in front of something that I would have to carry with me as long as I live: two men with no eyes, hanging from their legs. They were dead, probably from being dragged on the roads before they could meet their final punishment. Although they were dead, the Taliban still hung them in front of the public.

There were four or five Talibs with long beards, eyes with dark eyeliner, and long, black dresses. They walked back and forth, but nothing could distract me from the horror that cost me my soul and my childhood to see. I could not take my eyes off those faces with no eyes.

Soon more girls and boys found their way to the circle where the dead bodies were hanging. "This is not for kids, leave!" I heard the voice say a few times. I was afraid, so why couldn't I leave? Because it was too late; the image was sharp in my mind.

Eventually, the adults started to leave and I was no longer being pushed back and forth. As the adults left, the number of children increased. The Talib pointed a gun at two kids standing next to me and yelled again, "Go home!"

I had to run back home, but where was home? I passed many doors, roads, and alleys without stopping for a break. I had to find Nana. Then I could see the tall white walls of the mosque; home was near. I knocked on our door with the little strength left in me after running in the hot afternoon. "Coming!" Latif opened the door and said no more words after seeing my terror. I didn't look at her and ran to the living room, where I found Nana napping.

I sat in the corner of the room and stared at the ground. I gasped for air. I needed air before Nana was woken up by my breathless sounds. "What is wrong with you again?" Latif asked. "Why are your shoes around your waist? Where is your Siparah?"

Where was my Siparah? Where was Ranjita?! I always thought that I would never leave her behind in a bad situation. But I couldn't go back.

"Did the dogs chase you again, or the boys?" Latif asked, trying to get words out of my mouth, which had never been shut like this before.

That night was one of the hardest nights for me to sleep. I felt better in the morning when Nana's voice woke me up. But I had peed on the mattress during the night. "Wake up pee princess!" Latif demanded. Hearing my family's voices and seeing everyone moving around made me feel so much better.

"Stop it, Latif," Nana said, saving me from Latif. But I didn't need to be saved in that way. I understood a greater meaning of fear now.

I got ready for the mosque without having Nana or Latif scream at me to leave the house. I stopped by Ranjita's home and knocked nonstop. My concerns made me so impatient. Then Ranjita's father opened the door. "Hi, Sonita! Ranjita!

Sonita is waiting for you." I felt relieved, happy that she wasn't lost after all. I couldn't wait to see her.

"Are you done with Siparah yet?" her father asked me.

"No, I am still learning Siparah," I said.

"You know, I have already told Ranjita whenever she starts the Quran, I will buy her a gift," her father said. "But now I want to declare a new deal: I will reward whichever of you two finishes Siparah first." He didn't know that our biggest wish was to escape the mosque every day.

Then I saw Ranjita; she was okay. She didn't look upset and walked with me toward the mosque. "Where did you go yesterday?" asked Ranjita. I was happy that she hadn't seen what I had seen, and I had no interest or the courage to share.

Two or three days passed, and I was what Nana and Baba dreamed of—a "good girl." I didn't play outside, I tried to help Latif and Zia with housework, and I didn't wish to escape from or leave the mosque.

Then, one day, after having a nice breakfast of hot homemade naan with jam and butter, Ranjita and I made our way to the mosque, where the boys shared the rumors that they had seen the Akhund breaking off a branch from a tree. This meant that today he was going to try his new weapon on some or all of us. There was no way to escape—our absence could only make it worse, so Ranjita and I entered the crowded room.

"Sit down somewhere!" the Akhund said to me and Ranjita. Since we were already in God's favorite place, the mosque, I asked God not to let the Akhund turn into a monster again.

"Do you think I forgot the day you escaped the mosque to

go swimming? Do you?" the Akhund screamed. He received no response from any of us. We all fidgeted. I told myself not to panic because he had not seen me or Ranjita at the river that day. "I don't think he is going to even remember the boys he named," I whispered to Ranjita to make her feel safer. "Don't worry."

"Sonita, sit next to Zarin, now!" said the Akhund angrily. "Quiet everyone. Reza, come to me. You don't need your Quran." This was the first time that I heard him speak instead of screaming.

Reza was the skinniest boy in the mosque. He was the Akhund's favorite because he was always so honest and he was the second person who was able to finish the Siparah and start the Quran. "Well, I am glad to see you back and feeling better. Do you know, Reza, your father has given me permission to punish you if you misbehave?" asked the Akhund. "Do you know that?"

Reza shook his head.

"I can't hear you!" said the Akhund, as he was taking off the twigs on the branch.

"Yes, Akhund Sahib [respectable teacher]!" said Reza.

"But we can make a deal: tell me who else was with you on that day at the river so you can escape the punishment," said the Akhund. Suddenly all heads went down so they didn't make eye contact with the Akhund and Reza. Reza was still silent, staring at the ground. There was no way out for him. Finally, he pointed at a guy who was often with him in the mosque or by the Karbar.

The Akhund beckoned him. "No, no Siparah is needed, just bring yourself," said the Akhund as the first sinner took his initial and risky steps toward him. He sat by Reza, awaiting his punishment or wishing that he could punch Reza in the face. Then Reza pointed his finger at Shir Khan and, with his sad face, picked a few more. "How about girls?" asked the Akhund.

Now I was super nervous. What if he pointed to Ranjita or me? Then he picked Ranjita; I couldn't believe it! "He's lying, she was in class," I screamed, not knowing I could make things worse.

Then Reza pointed at me. "She was there too!" Suddenly I felt too weak to even show objections. *Stupid Reza*, I thought.

"You are lying, even in front of me and in this sacred place!" said the Akhund. "Come here, both of you!" Ranjita and I joined the big line of sinners. I looked at Ranjita, watching her playing with her fingers to distract herself.

Shatalagh! Everyone heard the first hit. Then the second hit. "Akhund Sahib, please forgive me!" Reza's friend begged for mercy, but the Akhund responded with the last hit—*Shatalagh!*

"Next time it might be even worse, so do not repeat it!" said the Akhund, watching the boy cry and clean his tears and nose on his sleeve. After him, Shir Khan crawled forward and sat on his heels, exactly in front of the Akhund. Shir Khan slowly put his hands up to receive his punishment. One hit, two! The third hit made him cry like the previous boy.

"Maybe by the time it is our turn, the stick will break," I whispered to Ranjita. "Or maybe he is going to be tired from beating all of us today."

But it was Ranjita's turn. She was already crying, probably from fear. "Sit here and put your sleeves up," said the Akhund. She sat in front of him, where he could see his target better.

Ranjita was wearing the shirt that I loved most. Now she struggled with it; the silky fabric of her long sleeves slipped down and covered the Akhund's target.

"Just put your hands together, your palms facing up," the Akhund said, rushing to be done with his performance. *Shatalagh!* The first lash made Ranjita cry harder. She put her hands in between her legs and hoped for a break before the next hit.

"Don't move your hands, or you will receive more!" said the Akhund.

Shatalagh! The second hit was done before the first could be endured. The boys had stopped crying, so now it was mostly Ranjita's cries that filled the room. The Akhund moved her small hands where he wanted them and raised his stick for the third hit. *Shatalagh!* Ranjita cried louder, and then to everyone's surprise, she yelled at the Akhund the phrase I taught her, "Fuck your mother!"

After a brief silence, almost everyone began to giggle. Some boys smiled wide even as their tears were still dripping on their cheeks, on their clothing, and on the ground. She spoke for all of us!

The boys and girls laughed while the Akhund ran around, mumbling nonsense things under his breath. He was probably searching for a stronger weapon for someone small, who said big and forbidden words.

I was experiencing a unique feeling. What was this? I couldn't express it, but in every Bollywood movie, people would say it to someone who did something great, something heroic. I even practiced it once to be ready to say it to Nana. It started with *E—efte . . . eftekhar!* Proud! Since Nana and Baba had never said it to any of us, this word was not part of our daily vocabulary. "*Be to eftekhar mikonam* [I am proud of you]!" I wanted everything to end soon so that I could say this to Ranjita!

"Quiet!" The room was once again back under the Akhund's

control. Finally, he found what he had been looking for: his hat and vest. "Everyone go home now!" The whole class rushed toward the small door that could hold only two people at once. It became clogged with the punished and the unpunished, all hoping to make it out of the mosque first.

Ranjita and I made brief eye contact and then ran to get our belongings so we could be the next people to escape. "Not you, Rejita," said the Akhund, mispronouncing her name, as always. "You are taking me to your house." He grabbed her hand and rushed to take her to her parents. He was probably going to ask her father to consider a greater punishment for her. But I wasn't scared; I knew that her parents would never physically punish her. Ranjita's mom was against the way Nana disciplined us. Ranjita was going to be returned to safe hands.

5

The Taliban at Our Home

One morning, a pain in my eyes woke me up earlier than usual. I couldn't open them. At first, I felt as if I were blind. Then, with each attempt to open them, I could feel one of my eyelashes pulling off. I followed the voices coming from our front yard and called for help.

Nana asked Latif to help me wash my face. "Here, you can have my tea; it's warm," Nana said. Latif washed my infected eyes with warm leftover black tea that smelled of cardamom.

"Eww! This is so gross!" Latif whispered as if she were scared of raising her voice. "Stop going to the dirty river, so you won't come back every day with a new disease. Nana hasn't slept since last night, so you have to be careful not to add to her frustration, Miss Sonita." They worried for Razeq, who had been at a party all night and hadn't returned home.

Finally, light found its way into the corner of one eye. I squirmed as Latif patiently worked on my other eyelid and listened to the noisy joy of children outside our yard's four walls, wanting to join them. Ranjita was probably waiting outside for me.

Suddenly, the sound of children's games vanished. Latif

rushed to look through the small hole in our door to check who was outside.

"Who is it?" Nana asked Latif with excitement. "Is it Razeq?"

"I can't really see anyone," Latif said. I blinked a few more times and saw my sister standing at the door on her toes, trying to see. I could hear the footsteps of a few adults walking toward our door.

"It's the Taliban!" Latif said. Nana abandoned her hookah in the kitchen, and then we heard a loud banging on the door.

"Stay there, don't panic!" said Nana quietly as she moved toward the door. "We've done nothing wrong." She was only a few feet away when someone kicked in the door. A group of Talibs forced themselves inside the yard, dragging a person who looked like Razeq behind them.

I screamed over cries of Nana and my sisters. I have never felt as unsafe as I did seeing the Taliban in our home.

I could hardly recognize Razeq. His black hair was gone, and there were scars on his scalp from being shaved carelessly. One of his eyes was swollen, half of his face was bruised, and he had no shoes or shirt on.

The men made their way into the yard and left Razeq lying on the wall. Scarier than the sight of Razeq were the Taliban: tall, shrouded in long black fabric, with strange black eyeliner around their eyes and guns on their shoulders. They were nothing like us. They could barely speak our language.

Nana ran toward Razeq, but they prevented her from getting close to his motionless body. When she tried to fight back, one of the men pushed her to the ground. Terrified, Latif ran toward the Talib who had pushed Nana, hitting him with the little strength that she had. How brave of Latif to even touch them, I thought. But my sister found herself on the ground next to Nana. As she stood up to go for another try, another Talib shot at the ground near her to stop her.

Screaming and shaking, I watched Nana try to stand up. Another blink, and I could see spots of cigarette burns on Razeq's arms. They looked fresh, as if he'd been tortured minutes before he was forced to bring them to our home.

"What have they done to you?" Nana asked Razeq.

The tall Talib moved toward Nana, warning her about raising her voice. "Your son has admitted that he stole a few items last night," said one of the men, who sat against the wall, playing with his gun while looking at Nana. "We must check the house." The others spread around the yard.

We watched as they walked through the hall, the kitchen, and downstairs. Fear weakened Nana; she no longer had the energy to try to stand up against them. "These are our belongings," Nana said repeatedly as the Taliban carried out dishes, clothing, home decorations, and Nana's sewing machine. They even took a full bag of rice that Baba had purchased for the winter.

"These items must be other people's belongings," the Talib said, emphasizing each word. They searched the basement and discovered that one of the rooms—Razeq's—was locked. "We need to check this room," said one of the Talibs. I couldn't breathe.

Nana was still on the ground not able to move or say a word. Razeq was awake now, and the Talib demanded again, "I said to unlock the door!"

"I can't. I don't have the key to open it," Nana said.

"Are you trying to hide something?" asked the short Talib standing by, ready to break the lock.

"No, we don't have the key," Nana responded.

"Well, too bad. Now we have no choice but to break the door."

The moment the Taliban turned their backs to walk toward the door, Razeq quietly stood up, using the wall for support. Nana knew his plan and did not try to stop him. Either way, he was going to be severely punished. If he were to escape, he'd have to stay away until their regime was a part of Afghanistan's dark history.

Suddenly Razeq ran as if he had saved all his energy for that moment. "He is gone!" yelled one Talib, as Razeq jumped on our outdoor oven.

Nana ran to help him, but he was already on the tall, thin wall of our property, walking slowly on its edge. He was a few steps away from the roof, which was connected to all of the other houses in the neighborhood, when—BANG!—the first bullet was released. I closed my eyes, covered my ears, and sat down, screaming again from the fear and the shock.

The rest of the men rushed out of the house to try to catch my brother. The shooter aimed at him for the second time. Nana ran toward him to prevent him from shooting, but he shot a second and third time.

I looked back; Razeq wasn't there anymore. Was he dead? Did he make it?

No, he didn't. He was screaming from the other side of the wall, "My hand, my hand!" The Talibs dragged him back inside the yard without paying any attention to his injuries. Blood from his forehead covered his face.

When the Talibs made sure that Razeq wasn't going to escape again, they broke into his room. They shattered his mirror, and once they saw everything in the colorful world of his room, items forbidden by the regime—photos and posters, a tape player with a stack of well-worn cassettes, love letters from Marjan—they assured each other that Razeq should not be killed alone.

"The punishment for all of you shall be death!" shouted one Talib.

I imagined the punishment for disobeying the Taliban's laws was something more terrifying than death by bullets, which killed right away. Something more like what I'd seen the other day.

Within minutes, the room was empty and the posters that carried signs of life and freedom for Razeq were gone. The men put valuable items aside in the corner of the yard. They broke all the cassettes; they tore apart the letters, though they couldn't read any of them. They made a big pile of all the *haram*, or forbidden, things in the middle of the yard.

I felt like time had come to a stop. Terrified, I hoped for everything to come to an end—even if it meant our lives.

Latif cried silently, trying to comfort me in her arms. Nana was still looking at Razeq and couldn't stop tearing up. The Talibs set the posters on fire in the middle of the yard with all of us around it. I saw the flames rising, reflected in Razeq's eyes as they threw in Marjan's love letters. Razeq's dreams fed the fire, but his eyes were dry: he was unable to cry anymore. The flames grew larger and stronger as the Talibs added notebooks, magazines, and drawings.

Suddenly Nana stood up and announced, "That is my daughter's room! She fled to Iran with her husband to escape this hell! You can't punish my kids because of her."

Nana concealed the truth behind lies, but even that would not ensure our safety. No matter whose room it was, the existence of *haram* created an opportunity for the Taliban to practice their cruelty and showcase their power.

"In no religion does God find pleasure in punishing an innocent," Nana cried. "Where is justice? Where is mercy? Where is God?"

This mention of God interrupted these godless people, and then they all took turns playing the boss. One of them slowly approached Nana, grinding his teeth. He stood over her and delivered his words in Pashto, a language that no one in my family spoke.

"There is no other religion but Islam, and if God was not present at this moment, I would voluntarily end your life," added another Talib, as he put aside a bag he'd found in the room.

"Go outside, wait by the alley," Nana whispered in my ear cautiously. "If you see your father and brother, tell them to stay at Uncle Ghani's house until we meet them."

I wished I could just stay inside. I didn't want to get close to the door. I repeated to myself, "Nana needs your help, Nana needs your help" and then ran out of the house. I saw the Taliban's truck parked on the street at the end of the alley. I looked around and through my tears saw a figure.

It was Shir Khan, the neighborhood bully. Seeing him at the end of the alley gave me a sense of security, even though he always excluded me from neighborhood games. How brave he was to be there while God himself was absent! Knowing he was seated there gave me the courage to continue toward the truck. As I began to leave the alley, I ordered him in my head, "Watch for me."

I passed the Taliban's truck; each of its wheels stood as tall as me. I started to run in my bare feet and stopped at a house a few blocks away, at the corner of a crossroads. From there, I could still see the truck, but only the back bumper. I sat down on the stairs of a house on the corner and looked to my left and right. I was alone. The street was as deserted as it was during curfew time.

"Are you okay?" someone asked quietly. I looked around for the speaker. "Look up, I'm here." She was familiar. I had seen her before around the mosque or maybe in the public showers. "Are you hurt?" she asked.

Was I okay? I was sick before the Taliban broke into our house, and after seeing them I was terrified—even scared of myself. I was scared of everyone; I was scared of the walls around me. Now my mind was becoming sick.

I looked at my house, at thick, black smoke finding its way to the sky from my house. *What is burning now?* I thought, crying and watching. *Is it paper or bodies?*

Someone turned on the truck, and I watched them from a block away. I saw two Talibs with Razeq's unconscious body, dropping him near the car.

Was he alive? *No God, please God! Please prove me wrong! Tell me that they are not going to drag him behind the car!*

Suddenly the men reappeared with carpets, rugs, and blankets in their hands. After organizing in the back of the big truck all that they'd stolen from our house, they each grabbed a part of Razeq's body and pulled him in.

The truck was now loaded with our belongings and my brother. About five of them with guns behind their backs sat around his body as the truck left our neighborhood. Once I couldn't see it anymore, I ran toward the house, anxiety forcing my legs to the broken door. I couldn't hear anyone talking or crying. I was scared of my own house.

"Come here!" I heard Latif. She was in the corner of the

yard, with Zia smooshed next to her. She opened her arms and held me so tight. It was crazy how much I felt better once I was in her arms. Until that day, I had never realized how much I loved Latif, Zia, Nana, Razeq, Baba . . . my family.

"She will be back soon," Latif said, after seeing me looking for Nana. I saw how the terror had paralyzed Latif and Zia, who were staring at the last flames burning the cassettes.

Days went by without any news from Razeq. Every day Nana paid a *falgir* (fortune teller) to tell her about his situation. Each one told Nana a different story. One said that his jinns (genies) told him that Razeq is okay. But I thought that was so wrong. The Taliban would not let him be okay. Another *falgir* had jinns who said that Razeq would return home in a few days. But a few days passed, and he did not come home.

One morning, Nana pulled me out of bed. "Why the rush?" I asked. "Where are we going?" My questions were left unanswered as Nana rushed us outside, where Baba was waiting. Like always, Baba was running his fingers through his *tasbih*, repeating God's ninety-nine names under his breath.

"Hold Baba's hand," Nana told me. Once again, I was chosen to be Baba's cane, to help him walk. I held Baba's hand, and he trusted wherever I put my steps.

The sky was the night's lightest blue; only a few of the brighter stars remained shining. Just the sound of wild dogs could be heard. Even though the sun was still asleep, there was enough light on the roads.

We walked until the sun appeared. Just when I felt that our destination would never be reached, Nana stopped in front of a long, tall building with barbed wire all around it. In front of the big iron door were three Talibs with guns in their hands. They were strolling around, protecting whatever was inside the four big walls.

Nana pointed to a car. "There he is. This is his car—right, Sonita?" Nana asked me to see whether one of the men was Faize. I stood up to see the man who was the driver.

"No, he is a Talib, not Uncle Faize," I whispered to Nana, who right away proved me wrong. A man with a long black dress, with black eyeliner around his eyes and a *tasbih* like Baba's in his hands, approached us and greeted Nana. "Salaam, Naser's mother and Mullah Payandeh." He sounded like Faize. But I still couldn't believe that he could be Faize; he hated the Taliban more than Razeq. Now he was one of them?

The moment Faize got closer to us, people began to fidget. Some conversations were dropped, some young people stopped laughing, and women hid behind their men. I was scared of him too.

Faize then gave Nana a bag. She hid it under her burqa, held her hand, and followed Faize to the iron door.

"Hello, brother, I'm here by the request of Habib Sahib," said Faize to one of the Talibs, who ran inside. Soon he came back and ordered the other Talibs who were guarding the door to let us in. "He is on the second floor in the farthest building," the Talib told Faize.

As we walked, almost all the Talibs who passed by greeted Faize with respect. "*Asalamu alaikum*, brother [hello, brother]." Then Faize walked faster toward a figure standing on the stairs. The Talib named Habib Sahib seemed to know Faize and opened his arms for Faize to greet him.

"Meet my brother, Mullah Payandeh," said Faize to the

Talib who seemed to be the boss. "We are here to—" Habib cut off Faize's sentence and told us to follow him upstairs. He guided us to a room where Razeq was seated on a chair. "Is this him?" Habib asked.

There he was, my brother, with a bruised eye and his hand tightened to his neck. I always thought that Baba disliked Razeq, but I saw how his eyes recognized his son right away, and he smiled. He was so happy. I couldn't tell how Nana was feeling. All I could hear was her quiet sobbing under the burqa. Razeq was looking at all of us but said nothing. He had lost weight; his black hair had started to grow back.

"Here is what I promised you, Habib Sahib." Faize took the bag from Nana and gave it to Habib, who opened it, put the bundles of money on the desk, and began to count. Razeq and I stared at it. It was the first time we'd ever seen so much money.

"Father, you appear to be a man of integrity and a good Muslim. Make sure that he does not end up here again," Habib said to Baba. "Otherwise, next time, he will have to pay with his life." Then he told us to leave.

Faize held Razeq's shoulder and took him down the stairs. Baba, Nana, and I followed them. I walked faster up to Razeq and held his hand. He looked at me and smiled, saying, "Gentle." Finally, he'd said a word. I wasn't sure what he meant until I felt the scabbed wound on the back of his thumb. I let go of his hand so my love wouldn't cause him pain.

Faize helped Razeq sit in the back of his car where Nana and I sat. Nana gave Razeq a big hug once the doors of the car were closed.

"I didn't steal anything," he said. "I was just with my friends singing." He began to cry alongside Nana, who had not asked for an explanation.

"May God make all your dreams come true, Faize," said Nana to Faize, thanking him for saving Razeq's life.

"We owe you so much," Baba added.

"I did it because I cannot lose my buddy," said Faize as he looked at Razeq in the rearview mirror.

"How many days do we have until we move out?" Baba asked Faize.

"Don't worry, you can stay there until you have a place to move to," Faize said.

It was then that Razeq and I understood where all the money had come from. Baba had sold our house—the only thing that we had to sell to flee to Iran. Now how would we be able to go to Iran?

Razeq was weeping even more now, blaming himself for everything. "Why would you give those motherfuckers even one Afghani?" Surprisingly, Baba wasn't upset with Razeq using bad words.

"House in exchange for your life—I think it is a good deal, Razeq," Faize said. He told his cousin to stop sobbing and be happy he was still alive.

6

Becoming a Thief

Razeq could have recovered much sooner if the news of Marjan being forced into marriage had not reached him. But after a few days went by, and he was able to walk and speak again, he asked me to go with him to the old neighborhood. "That is such a nice plan, why don't you two have some *shur nakhud* [chickpeas with spice and vinegar] on your way?" said Nana.

Unlike other days, Razeq did not speak of Marjan as we walked. But he asked me if I had started studying the Quran. I told him no and that I didn't go to the mosque anymore. He put his hand on my shoulder and tapped on it as a sign of contentment, saying, "Kokosto, you gave me the best news!" Razeq approved of my misbehavior once again.

After passing by several blocks, we arrived in our old neighborhood. Razeq approached a few boys, who were happy to see him. No one asked what had happened to his hair and face, as if his friends all knew his story. Once Razeq was among his old friends, he seemed so happy and playful.

We went back to the neighborhood many times until Baba said that Razeq had regained his lost energy and had to return to work. Soon the little money that was left from selling our house was given to an old couple who sold us their house.

Our new house had two rooms. The windows had no glass, so heat and cold entered the rooms and our bones. The only door was the entrance. The bathroom had a curtain instead of a door; the kitchen was probably the only part that was similar to our old house.

I'd left our old house with sadness after I couldn't find Ranjita to say goodbye.

War brought more poverty and insecurity. Baba didn't want Razeq, Naser, Khaleq, and Zaher to search for work outside the house because they could be taken by the Taliban to be turned into soldiers. He'd heard of this happening at the mosque before he quit attending. As Baba said to Nana and my brothers, "If the Taliban wants you to join them, they will ask you one simple question: 'Are you a Muslim?' If you say yes, you will be assigned to fight on the front line, which means you will be killed by the people fighting the Taliban. If you say no, they will kill you for not being Muslim."

Since the men could not work, Nana had to go to the marketplace with Zaher to sell gasoline to lazy drivers who didn't want to stand in long lines to get fuel for their vehicles. I missed the old days hearing the arguments between Zia and Latif over preparing breakfast, lunch, and dinner; we even had brunch sometimes.

One day, playing outside with the doll Latif had made for me, I found a broken stick and began to practice writing my name the way Ranjita had taught me. I was missing her as much as I was missing the good old days.

Then a big shadow appeared on my head. "Please help me, give me some bread and rice," the old beggar asked, as I looked at her bag full of bread and other edible things.

"We have no bread or rice," I said, tempted to ask *her* for some bread. She saw my bare feet and dusty skin, playing alone, so she left to find someone else. I watched her as she walked away and knocked on other doors. Thoughts of following her path began to move my legs toward the doors of our neighbors. I moved behind her with curiosity, learning from her how to kindly ask for help. Then I began to do the same.

My first knock drew the attention of the beggar, who wasn't happy to see a competitor in the poorest area of town. From the other side of the alley, she looked at me not with surprise, but with anger, as if it were her area of business. I would ignore the doors she knocked on and move to the next door.

I could walk faster than she could, which was to my benefit. I knocked on all the doors that I came to. Most people didn't open their door after hearing my request for some bread, and some of them opened their door and told me to go away and knock on others. At the next house, someone opened the door and gave me a piece of bread. I walked a few houses away, sat in a shaded place, and ate the whole piece of bread in a few minutes, but I still felt hungry.

I realized that I liked begging—it was much easier than waiting around for Nana to bring food. I continued on this path, not knowing where it would end up. I walked nonstop, knocking on all the doors until exhaustion took over. I sat down and realized that I had collected a big bag of bread that could feed all of us for that night or even the next morning for breakfast.

I looked around, not knowing where I was, but not too far away I saw something like a marketplace. I walked toward the busyness, and soon I lost the old beggar. But now there were many of them spread among the cars, stores, and fruit vendors.

I couldn't remember the last time we had had grapes in our house. Baba loved the juicy Fakhri grapes, which were sweet, but not too sweet. They were my favorite too. It had been so long since I had seen Fakhri in the market, but they were in almost every fruit shop.

I took my steps toward the closest shop and said, "Please help me, I haven't had anything to eat today." I repeated the sentence that I had learned from other beggars nearby. Without saying a word, the shopkeeper took his flyswatter and swatted me away from the fruit. Not knowing the consequences of stealing, my hands went toward the grapes and took as many as they could grab. Holding tight to my bag of bread, I ran away. As I was running, I put one grape in my mouth and chewed. I swallowed the sweetness of the grape—which was followed by an unfamiliar pain.

The owner of the fruit shop had grabbed me by my hair and slapped me with all his strength. The sound of the slap interrupted the sellers, customers—old and young—all the beggars, and the Taliban who were in the market strolling around. I fell to the ground, not knowing where I was, why people circled me, and why I wasn't moving to leave the scene.

"You little bitch, did you think you could run away from me?" The shopkeeper's voice brought me back to myself. I sat crying and looking for a way to escape, but his words had attracted a circle of men and old beggars. As a few of them left the circle, I saw a possible way to escape; I stood up and ran as fast as I could.

The owner of the shop was no longer inclined to stop me. What else could he possibly want from me? I paid him with tears and pain, I paid him with everything that I had, nothing and everything at once.

The sound of the slap rang in my head. I ran, ran, and ran until I lost the shopkeeper—and then myself. I sat down somewhere away from the marketplace and began to cry—not because my bare foot was wounded, not because one side of my face still felt numb from the sudden blow, but because I had lost the bag of bread. I had thought I could feed my family that night.

I ran most of the deserted alleys before it was too late to find home. On my way, I found a mosque where I could drink some water. I entered the mosque, began to drink, and washed my face. I could hear the voices of kids reading the Quran and Siparah. I walked closer to the doors and looked at the slippers, which were all boys' shoes. I tried one pair that wasn't too big and left the mosque.

When I got home, the door was locked. I was so tired. I knocked until I heard footsteps.

Zia, looking at my new slippers, asked, "Can I try them?" I left the slippers near her feet and ran toward Nana's voice. "Where have you been?" she asked. "Razeq almost ate your piece of *qalef*!" Nana gave me the piece of *qalef* on the corner of the tablecloth. She was happy; everyone's face was happier than how I had seen them in the morning. Latif was drinking tea with *qalef* alongside everyone else.

"So then what happened?" Naser asked Nana with excitement.

"So, the businessman Mr. Mubin bought the last barrel of gasoline before the Talib could confiscate it, handed us the bag of bread and *qalef*, and took us to his beautiful house where we did cleaning," Nana said. "He thinks I'm a great cook!"

I put some *qalef* in my mouth and enjoyed the sweetness of the forgotten taste. It tasted better than Nana's *qalef*, or maybe hunger had given everything a new taste—even a piece of bread, a new taste.

Nana opened the bag of bread again, giving each of us an

equal amount. "This is for today and tomorrow; eat responsibly," she said. Zaher ate everything in an instant, as if there were no tomorrow. Nana knew that none of us would save any bread, but she said it anyway. That way, if the hunger came back earlier than usual the following day, we should not complain.

As the city was getting lost in the war, the job opportunities slowly faded away. After Nana lost her job, starvation forced us onto a field covered with opium poppy flowers, red, white, and purple. Amo, the old man who owned the farm, set two rules: do not cut the flowers, and do not eat anything on the farm. I liked the job already after seeing how much the field looked like Greenland across the Karbar but with flowers scattered wherever the eye could see.

"Remember, it's not the flowers that we want, it's the tears of the flowers, the *shahd* [sap] from the seed pods," said Amo. He took the knife from me and followed the marks I had made on the pods with my knife. "You are weak. You need to cut deeper, we don't want surface scratches," said the old man, who then left to check on the beginners expected to become masters the following day.

I put my sharp knife on the poppy seed pod and cut deep. The milky opium sap oozed out from the fresh incisions and sat on the surface of the pod. I wasn't sure if I did it right until the old man said, "That is better, now move to the next one."

After cutting a few pods, I felt better about my job. I was good at cutting since I had practiced it on the stomachs of fish that Ranjita and I had caught and cooked. Unlike other children in the field, I wasn't scared of holding a knife.

"You two, out of the field now!" Amo fired two of the children who seemed not as serious as the adults. The job was very easy, but it was hard to be strong to say no when another child invited you to play.

"Once the sun sets, return all your tools to where you got them," said Amo. Everyone had to be in the field before the sun would touch the field, and everyone had to be out of the field after the sun left. In between, we had breaks—not for playing, but for lunch and using the bathroom.

Despite the mosquitoes, I slept well. Not because I went to bed with a full stomach, but because of working from early in the morning until late afternoon. The next day Amo gave Zia and me spoons and cups and sent us back to the field, telling us, "Use only the spoon to collect the opium sap; don't use your fingers." After the first week, Latif made a friend. They exchanged stories, laughed, took their breaks together, and enjoyed the weather after the harsh conditions for cooking.

Work was getting harder on the hot days. Amo started to charge us more for our room than he had before we started working, and he often tried to make Razeq smoke with him. Latif suggested that we leave, but Nana stayed and worked in the field until the last day of the opium harvest.

When there were no unscarred poppy seed pods to be found, Amo assumed that it was the end of the harvest. He gave us the leftover money and told us goodbye. We all thought of walking back to the city on foot, but it would be dark before we arrived. So we found a van, Nana did the bargaining, and the driver agreed to have me and Zia ride for free. I sat on Nana's lap, Zia sat on Latif's lap, and we headed to the city. We weren't the only people in the van with extremely sunburned faces and hands dyed black from opium sap after two weeks in the fields.

No one questioned what our job was; we all looked like farmers, so it didn't matter what we cultivated. We walked the alleys to our house. Unfortunately, we were welcomed home with bad news: Baba was sick. We had no choice but to use the money we had made to take Baba to see a doctor.

I was surprised by how the feeling of hunger had turned me into a lawbreaker and fearless person. I no longer paid attention to the laws made by my family and the Taliban; the only thing I knew was my desire to find food. After several tries, I got good at something bad. I was only about five years old.

I would leave the house and come back with bags full of bread, biscuits, chocolate, fruit, and other foods that I stole and could fit in the bag. I wasn't scared of being caught; I was scared of hunger. Although Nana often warned us against stealing, now she admired my skills. Baba was the only one unaware of my misbehavior.

I put everything I stole in the kitchen, out of sight. How funny of Baba that he would eat the bread I stole, use the cleaning supplies I stole, and yet would not ask where they came from. He probably believed that God had brought them to our house. God even took credit for my work.

Every day I left home in the morning and returned in the afternoon with the food I stole. It never crossed my mind to steal something for myself. But once, when I saw a store that had my favorite doll, which Nana had never gotten for me, I began strategizing how to steal it.

It was better than Ranjita's doll. She would close her eyes when I laid her down. Her blond hair was so shiny and soft that I couldn't stop stroking it—until the owner of the store told me to put the doll down and leave. He was worried that my dusty, dirty hands would put a black mark on the doll's hair.

Outside the store, I waited for it to get busier so I could blend in with customers. I walked into another super-crowded store, put a scarf on my head and found a jacket, put it on, and left the store. Then I walked between a few women walking toward the toy store, blending in between a woman and an old man. I walked so close to the women that the shop owner probably thought I was with my mother. I got to the doll, but she was a little hard to reach. When I stretched to grab her, she fell to the floor. When my eyes met the owner's, I grabbed the doll and ran.

I heard the shop owner screaming, "*Duzd, duzd* [thief, thief]!" As his screams got closer, I slowed down before the Taliban or someone could arrest me. I walked slowly into a clothing store and pretended to be one of the customer's children. When I saw the owner run by the store, I took my scarf, put it around the doll, and walked outside. When I was out, I ran in the opposite direction from the owner of the toy shop toward home. I was sweating underneath my jacket, but I didn't stop running—until I fell in the mud. My heart broke when I saw that the shiny golden hair of the doll was all muddy, and one of her eyes had broken.

When I got home, Nana saw the doll in my hand, but she liked the jacket better. "I'm glad that out of the ten of us, one got to prepare for winter."

In the morning a man Ata's age knocked on the door and asked for Nana. I knew him; he was the peddler who used to sit next to Nana and me when we were selling second-hand clothing.

"Welcome, Munis Jan. Please come in," Nana said. "Feel free to look around," she offered, as he was checking the kitchen, the bathroom, the common room.

"This is a very small house," said Munis. "Selling it would only get you closer to the Iranian border, not to Iran." He called himself a businessman, but he was bargaining on the price of the house as if it were a used shirt. Once he left, Nana went back to her hookah and began to cry. Knowing that she got headaches from crying too much, Latif started to massage her head: "Don't worry, God will help us to leave Afghanistan before winter is here." Everyone was scared that our house could collapse on our heads the moment winter arrived. Baba couldn't build a stronger roof since there was no money to purchase wood and other materials that would keep us safe from the cold Herat winter. We had to hurry.

The next day Nana took our blankets and carpets that had fewer holes and other items to the market to sell. The market was busier than before, with more than fifty rows of sellers. Everyone was screaming to get the shoppers' attention, rushing to sell their goods before the Taliban displaced them or the buyers ran out of money. Soon I joined the mixed voices and screamed, "Come get warm blankets, and a handmade carpet for a cheap price." I was able to attract a few buyers.

"Two hundred Afghani would be good?" asked one.

"Look at it again and feel it, you will not find a carpet like this in the market," Nana said. "The price is 350 Afghani."

"I have to pay more than its price to carry it home! How about 250 Afghani?"

"The final price is 350, and I will not reduce it."

"How about 260?"

"It is handmade and worth at least 290 Afghani," Nana said.

"I would pay if I had money, how about 270 Afghani?"

This was a conversation that would go on for what felt like hours until Nana or the buyer would run out of energy to bargain.

Suddenly Nana said, "I am also a *falgir* [fortune teller]. Do you want me to see your future?" This was the first time I heard Nana say such a thing.

"There are more *falgir* than buyers. Tell me one thing about me to show why you are the best *falgir*," said the buyer, who was an old man.

Nana, without thinking, said, "My jinns are telling me that you come from a faraway village, and have two wives."

The old man was so amazed that right after he heard Nana's guess, he sat down and asked, "Is your fortune-telling as expensive as your blankets?"

Although Nana guessed everything correctly, I was not super amazed: his accent showed that he wasn't from the city, and it was easy to guess that he had two wives. Most of the people we knew had two wives or were thinking of a second marriage.

Nana looked at the big gold ring on his finger and answered carefully. "I don't put a price on my fortune-telling; I tell you about your future, and you can give me whatever you can."

Scared that the crowd would hear him, the old man got closer to Nana and asked, "Do you have something for me to give my wives so they can become friends?"

"This should not be a problem, as I had a similar request a few days ago," said Nana. "But you must come in an hour when I have the right material and the wives' information to make your *taweez* [spellbinder]." Nana, who hated lying, forced her words through a shaky voice, grabbing the old man's attention.

"I will be here, Sister. My first wife's name is Soraya, twenty-four years old, and my second wife's name is Monira, nineteen years old. She is the troublemaker."

Nana had learned so much from *falgir* and *shikhs* in our town. After the old man left, I found a *tasbih*, as Nana asked.

She took two beads from it and put them on a thread. They looked so much like *falgirs'* spellbinders, which were so expensive, but Nana gave it to the old man an hour later and received a decent amount of money for two useless beads.

After several days, the last blanket that had kept us warm was gone for a cheap price. We had some money from selling the blankets, the rug, and Nana's new job as a *falgir*. Still, we were hungry and couldn't ignore our empty stomachs. Even though we had no goods to sell, every day Nana took me with her to the marketplace to sell news from the future.

People would come to Nana to give her money in exchange for a piece of paper, the *taweez*, that they believed was written by Nana's jinns. "Don't ever open the folded paper; it will have no effect once it is unfolded," Nana told old and young.

I was the one who cut and folded all the papers to sell them to people as *taweez*. If someone opened it, they would find out that nothing was written on it. Some days we had more people around our carpet than other merchants who were selling things that were real. But people liked Nana's words. She never put a price on her *taweez* and people thought that she was being honest.

I almost began to believe in Nana's fortune-telling when an old woman sat on our carpet and kissed Nana's hands. She had come crying to Nana a few days before, saying that her son had gone to Iran but she had no news of him. "I had a dream that his friends killed him on the way to take his money." The woman repeated this sentence to Nana, asking her to see her son's fortune.

Nana told her, "You don't have to pay, I will do it for free." She felt bad for the woman, and she did not want to take her money. "My jinns tell me that your son is safe in Iran. Do not be sad, he will return to you healthy and happy. And I have demanded my jinns to watch out for him."

The woman's cries turned to joyful laughs, and her other son smiled. They both left with smiles on their lips. That day I saw Nana selling hope to people for free.

When the woman returned a few days later, she said, "My son has made it to Iran safely." She handed *qalef* to Nana, saying, "May God bless you and your family." I may have been happier than the woman and Nana: I had *qalef*!

That day Nana gave many people good news. Whenever someone came to her, she sent them back with a big smile on their face. She sometimes did not accept money from people who looked as poor as we were.

She decided to call it a day before sunset. On the way back home, Nana bought saffron and a drawing notebook. She gave me the drawing notebook so I could draw for people who bought Nana's fortune-telling. Nana melted the saffron in warm water and mixed it until the liquid turned red. She burned a match, and once the tip of it turned sharp like a pencil, she gave it to me. "Dip the tip of the match into the saffron liquid and draw whatever you want on every other page," said Nana. I wasn't sure what her plan was, but I enjoyed drawing shapes that came across my mind. It didn't take me too long before I ran out of pages. I folded each page like Nana's other *taweez* and made them ready for whoever was going to buy them.

One day Nana had a bad cold and couldn't make it to the marketplace. To our surprise, her customers found our house. That's how Nana's secret was revealed to Baba.

Baba said nothing to Nana besides asking her to never use her magic to spread hatred. It was then that I thought Baba was one of the people who believed in Nana's imaginary power. She was successful at her job because she never set a price; she told people to give her whatever they could.

One day, I was in the room with Nana when a fat white lady came in, with several gold rings and a thick gold necklace. She sat close to Nana. "I used to be my husband's *nafas* [air to breathe], but now he barely notices me. I am here to get a *taweez* to make him love me again."

Nana listened and took a stick that I'd brought her from outside. She put the lady in the middle of the room and made a circle around her. She said words that no one could understand, and her customers all believed that she was talking to her jinns. After a few minutes, Nana gave the woman one of the drawings that I had made and told her to put it inside her husband's pillow.

People were satisfied with Nana's fortune-telling, but after that day, she stopped. Her lies got bigger and eventually haunted her. Like me, Nana was tired of doing bad things.

Soon Nana and I returned to the marketplace where we sold all our belongings, even my doll. Razeq and Naser received their wages. That night was the first in a long time when I saw Nana smile. We had a little more money than what Munis asked for to start our trip to Iran. Nana took half of it to him and came back with good news: we were going to leave Afghanistan in just two days.

It actually took more than two weeks to receive four days' notice and a place to meet Munis. That gave us time to sell the house for a price higher than Munis had offered.

On our last night, Zia refused to sleep. Instead, she stared at the sky for a long time, as if she had to say goodbye to all the stars.

7

"If You Don't Have Money, I'll Take Your Daughter"

When Munis picked us up in the morning, he took us through our old neighborhood, where I saw the Karbar. I stared at it until we drove too far away to see it anymore. I silently said my goodbyes. Goodbye, Ranjita; goodbye, Karbar. I hope we meet again.

As we requested, Munis took us to say goodbye to Aziz. When we arrived, she was already standing by the door with Ata and her kids. She was sobbing under her burqa. "I thought you left without a goodbye," she said. She still sounded mad at Nana and Baba for wanting to start a journey that seemed to be out of our reach.

"Winter is so close! Baba, Nana, don't do this to yourselves," Aziz repeated, even though her words were ineffective. Nana showed her the back of the car, which was filled with food and warm clothing, but Aziz was still worried.

"We have to leave!" Munis screamed for the second time. Nana rushed her goodbye and made her way back to the car. As the wheels began to turn, I put my head out of the window, waving until the car changed its direction.

Once we left the city, Munis, who was so tired of hearing cries, took a cassette tape from his pocket and played it. The moment Razeq heard it, he began to sing along to Ahmad Zahir. "*Sultan ghalbam, to hasti, to hasti* [you are the king of my heart, you are, you are]."

"Brother, you have a beautiful voice," Munis complimented Razeq, who was drowned in the joy of the music and couldn't hear him. Hours passed on the endless road, the sun burning directly on top of our heads. Zia and I put our heads outside and only stopped when other cars passed us.

Then a van pulled in front of us, the dust of the road forcing us to close all the windows. In just a few seconds, the van disappeared, and Munis complained to Baba about crazy new drivers. Soon the long road that seemed to be endless cut to the left, crossing between two big mountains. The moment we turned, the van that had passed us appeared again.

"Can't he see the road?" asked Razeq. "Why is he leading travelers into a trackless wasteland?"

Munis didn't answer Razeq's question because he wasn't sure what was happening. He slowed down and looked at the van. Suddenly the van turned on its hazard lights to warn our driver, and Munis immediately told everyone to hold tight, and he turned the wheel of the car. I wasn't sure what he was running away from until two Talibs who were hidden on the other side of the mountains stood up and pointed the gun at our car. Since there was no way to go back, Munis turned again. Seeing our car speeding up, one Talib shot at it. Munis slowed the car as a sign of surrender.

"Hide your money and jewelry," said Munis.

Baba began to argue. "Is this where you wanted to lead us, to the Taliban?" His screams were lost in the chaos. Nana opened the back of the tea flask and put some money in there and some under her scarf between her braids and made a big knot. Then she told Zia and Latif to get under the back seat so they wouldn't be raped or taken as wives. Razeq was still giving Munis directions to escape, but he didn't think there was a safe way out.

"They have guns, didn't you hear the bullets hitting the fucking car?" Munis screamed. I wasn't crying or screaming; I was lost in emotion, in terror. I wasn't sure what was happening.

The moment our car stopped, my heart began to beat faster. Two Talibs with guns pointed at us yelled words in Pashto. "He wants you all out of the car," Munis translated in an angry voice.

"Don't move!" Nana whispered to Zia and Latif as we left the car. I realized that I forgot to put my shoes on when the heat on the road burned my feet.

Two of the Taliban rushed to our car, two took a stand by the mountains where cars entered into their territory, and two of them stayed with us. They were no different from what we saw in the city—long black dresses, black eyeliner, and guns in their hands.

One Talib, who could speak Farsi, hit Munis in the face for not stopping the car sooner. He left him alone once he began to bleed from his nose and mouth. We all knew how cruel they were, but it was always shocking to see them carry out their cruelty in front of your eyes.

The second Talib, who spoke Pashto and Farsi, pointed his gun at us and demanded money. He pointed at Baba, saying, "First of all, I want that watch and the vest." Baba had no strength to fight the robbers, so he gave them what they asked for. "You, old man, the vest comes with whatever is inside its pockets, including money," said the Talib, who saw Baba take his *tasbih* from his pocket.

The Talib hit Baba in the stomach with the back of the gun and took his *tasbih*. Razeq and Naser rushed to hold Baba, who was in so much pain, but the Talib ordered both of them to stay where they were.

"You animals! Fight someone who is your age," said Razeq.

The other Talib, who was now in search of money and goods in the back of the car, ran and kicked Razeq on the back. He fell to the ground. Nana was crying louder than me. Khaleq and Zaher were sobbing in fear. We were all in a big circle, with one Talib in the middle and one in the back of the car, frustrated because they didn't find any money.

I wanted to scream for help, but there was no one there. People from another car that had been stopped earlier cried even louder than we did but still received no help. The Talib who spoke Farsi made his way to our car and looked at a few bags that were on the seats.

Like Nana, I was in terror: What if the Talib finds Latif and Zia?

"I only have this much money," Nana spoke up. To my surprise, her distraction worked. The Talib left the car and took the money.

"I know one thing: no one starts this long trip without money. But if you don't have money, fine, I'll take your daughter," said the Talib and made his way toward me. I felt so unsafe, even with all my family members around me.

"You touch her, and I will kill you, or you will have to kill me," Razeq said, after seeing how frightened I was. The Talib walked toward Razeq and put his foot on his head. He was probably about to stand on Razeq's head when gunshots stole his attention. A war between the robbers and some new travelers was happening in between the two mountains. The Talib who spoke only Pashto said something to the other Talib and ran toward where the shooting was happening.

"Sit down everyone," said the other Talib, who was assigned to watch us until his accomplice returned. He began to stroll in a circle, holding tight to his gun, and made Naser check everyone's pockets for money. When Naser got to Nana, the Talib said to him, "No need to check her; it looks like the only thing that she possesses is her daughter, so give me the little girl."

Naser refused. The Talib went to hit Naser for the second time, and Razeq grabbed the Talib by his feet and threw him to the ground. Naser took his gun from him and pointed it at the Talib. Razeq hit the Talib on his face, and blood found its way to the ground.

Until that day, I had never seen Razeq that angry. He hit him several times and said his usual sentence: "Fuck your mother, fuck you!"

It seemed that for the first time, we defeated the Taliban.

"Hit that motherfucker!" said Munis, who had a big smile on his wounded face. Munis ran to help Zaher and Khaleq put our belongings back in the car.

"To the car, now!" Razeq told everyone to leave the scene, took the gun from Naser, and pointed it at the Talib. "Without this gun, you're just a fucking coward," Razeq screamed at the motionless body and sobbed. I thought he was going to kill him, but he didn't. He gave the gun back to Naser, searched the Talib's pockets one more time, and ran to the car with Naser. "Let's go!"

The speed of the car took us so far that even the bullets shot by the Taliban on the wasteland could not reach us. We had won this time.

"Here you go, Baba," Razeq said, giving his watch and *tasbih* back to him. Baba was so happy and proud of Razeq for saving our lives.

"Brother, you made one of my biggest dreams come true: I always wished to see a defeated Talib," Munis said to Razeq. "A common dream, Munis," said Razeq, who began to empty his pockets of what he had stolen back from the Talib.

It turned out that he had stolen more than we ever had: one gold necklace, three gold rings, and a thick bracelet with four gold coins. "I wish I could see their faces when they return to see us gone and all the valuable items that they stole from others," said Razeq, as he kept looking at the gun. "That's an M16, isn't it?" asked Munis.

"I don't know, it's my first time holding a gun. It's pretty heavy," said Razeq.

In the late evening, we arrived at a place called Mehman Khaneh Zaghak. Razeq put the gun on his shoulder, just to be safe, and we all slept in one room together. Nana no longer tried to hide Latif from Munis. He was a respected man. The big room had two windows, which allowed the wind and mosquitoes to travel inside.

The best part of being there was the food. We had enough money that Nana and Baba allowed us to have more food if we were still hungry. "Tomorrow my partner, Ali, will drop us off at the endpoint for cars because they cannot climb the mountains," Munis said, once again checking out the gun. He tried to teach Razeq how to hold it properly, but Razeq showed no interest. Instead he ate and decided to call it a day.

We left before sunrise. The moment I sat by the car window,

next to Nana, I felt warmer and fell asleep. I woke up when we reached the endpoint. After Munis said goodbye to his partner and gave him the car, he told us to sit down and listen to him before we started to walk the last part of the journey.

"Wear two pairs of pants, and socks," said Munis while he fastened his shoelace. "Eat a big breakfast right now, and go through your belongings one more time, throwing away what might slow you down. We might be walking for five days."

We already knew it might be a long walk, but five days seemed like an impossible journey for Baba to take. "Now listen carefully," Munis said. "You can talk, you can breathe freely, until I raise my hand, which means absolute silence. Remember that we are uninvited guests," he added, reminding us of the police checkpoints.

The steep hills seemed risky for Baba to climb without any support, so as we began our journey, Munis assigned Naser to be Baba's guide. Although we were all breathing heavily, Munis climbed without complications, barely taking his eyes off his watch.

"We have to rush," Munis said, refusing to slow down. "If we lose the light of the day, there is only a small chance that all of us will make it to the other side of the mountain without falling or dealing with snakes." The fear of encountering snakes pushed us all to the top of the mountain sooner than Munis expected. Although he was so glad and feeling proud, we all felt disappointed to see the other side of the mountain: there was no village, just more unclimbed mountains.

"What is this?" Baba asked. "We walk the whole day to get to this mountain chain?" Exhaustion had stolen Baba's patience. Munis understood Baba's frustration and assured him that we were on the right track. We weren't lost.

As the sun began to set, our day came to an end. We had arrived in a place surrounded by mountains, small trees, and trash everywhere. "Are there any animals here?" I asked Munis, who laughed and said, "There are, but not more dangerous than humans."

Nana put a big blanket on the ground and one on the side to cover ourselves when we slept. The cold convinced Munis to make a fire. "Don't put on more wood, because we don't want to catch any attention," Munis said. "We are only twenty kilometers away from the first police checkpoint." Since we knew nothing about kilometers, Nana asked Munis to convert kilometers to hours. "Around five hours," said Munis.

After a quick and sufficient dinner, ten of us put the two blankets around ourselves and sat close to each other to prevent the cold from stealing the little heat between us.

When Munis and Nana woke us up in the morning, everyone felt pain in their muscles and joints. Like my family, I hadn't recovered from the day before, but a harder day began. We walked in the rain and strong winds. I wished we could walk on the flat road I saw instead of climbing mountains.

"There's a road over there, why can't we take it?" I asked Munis breathlessly. He told me to lower my voice. I guessed that if we were on the road, the police car that patrolled the area every day could easily see us. "The only place where we cannot be seen is between these mountains," said Munis, leading the way.

As the light of the day began to fade, we heard three police cars passing on the road. "That is the first Iranian police station," Munis said, pointing at a white building in front of the mountain. We survived walking in darkness and arrived at the place where we spent a second night.

Day five, day six, and even day seven passed without a sign of a destination. The fear of winter catching up with us forced everyone to walk faster.

By the end of day eight, the mountains began to flatten, which made walking easier but hiding harder. Sometimes we had to crawl instead of walk. Munis taught us how to safely crawl with all of our belongings on our backs. Nana and Latif could no longer carry their hijabs, so they left them on the ground and put a big rock on them to stop the wind from blowing evidence to the Iranian police.

When darkness came, we began to crawl in a line of ten people toward the light of the police checkpoint. Razeq was the last person in line because he had to help Baba. Each time we crawled, my hands got more and more wounded and hurt profoundly.

"*Chop!*" Munis ordered everyone to be silent and to quit crawling. "The car is leaving, you can breathe now." When Munis said that, I was probably the first person to sit up and give my chest and arms a break. I could see the red and blue lights of the car getting farther and farther away. The moon was hanging low, covered with clouds ready to cry over our heads.

I held Nana's hand and continued walking. It was past our bedtime, and I couldn't keep my eyes open. I closed them, just to give them a break, and had begun to fall asleep when a snowflake landed on my nose and woke me up. I held my head up; the second and third snowflakes landed on my cheeks, inside my eyes, and melted in one blink.

"Be quiet, don't move," said Munis when car headlights

between the trees lit up the area. For a moment we thought the police had found us. We ran between the trees but then heard Munis say, "Get inside the truck." We made our way back hesitantly. "Hurry up, there is no time, and hold on to the roof panel as tight as you can," said Munis as he helped Nana get on the bed floor of the truck.

The truck's driver, who was standing on its roof, looking all around, said, "*Mashin* Police, is coming toward us." *Mashin*, a car—the first word of Farsi that Ranjita had taught me. I felt something so strange that I cannot explain. Perhaps it was a moment of pride knowing what the word meant.

"Hold tight!" said Munis, who sat with Baba in the front seat. The moment the driver started the truck, the mighty power of the speedy truck slammed us all into the tailgate. My hand got crushed as I hit the wheel tube. I held myself to the roof panel with the other hand as the wind and snow tried to push me out of the truck. Once Naser held me, I rushed to take care of my hand, which felt painful even to hold it.

We were all in a panic, afraid of falling off the truck. It drove so fast that we didn't have a chance to save the bag that had our blanket and some of our clothing in it. From the speed of the snowy wind, my teeth began to bang into one another. The light of the police cars was so close. Suddenly the driver turned off the truck's headlights. Driving in the dark, we hit a pothole that broke the tailgate door.

"Hold on to the sides!" said Munis. The driver put down the windows, which gave Naser and Razeq something to hold on to. Slowly my uninjured hand began to weaken as the cold stole my body heat. *I'm going to be the next to fall off this truck*, I thought. But then the truck slowed down, and right away the driver turned it off and asked everyone to stay quiet.

Was this all for nothing? I asked myself, thinking of how far we'd walked, when the police car changed its direction. I was so happy to see it disappear.

Everyone began to breathe. We waited between the trees, snow slowly covering us. The driver and Munis argued about which way to go and when. I could understand only a little since many words in Persian were new to me. Finally, the driver left the spot without turning on the headlights and began to drive slowly. The truck struggled to drive over a few more potholes until we found the road.

We're going to live! I said to myself. I looked at the lights on the horizon, which brought us hope.

Finally, we made it to our destination! How happy I was to see everyone in my family alive after such a long and risky ride! The driver led the way to a room that was warm enough to melt the ice in our blood. The house was big, but the driver told us that we weren't allowed to leave the room unless we had to use the bathroom.

For dinner, the driver brought us yogurt and naan. Once Munis was done eating, he asked the driver for a cigarette. Munis lit it up and told the driver to be extra cautious with Baba because of his age. "From here, Qasem will take care of you," Munis said to us. "He knows Zabul like the palm of his hand. He will drive you to Mashhad. No extra cost. I always do the walking, and he takes it from here."

Nana thanked him for risking his life to help us.

"This is my job. If not you, I will risk my life for another traveler who can pay the amount. Thank you, Razeq, for saving my life," said Munis. He gave Baba and my brothers a hug, took his blanket, and went to his room.

In the morning, I woke up to Qasem's loud and annoying

voice. "*Waqt raftaneh*, it's time to go! Wear this clothing in case we might need to walk. It is better to disguise yourself—you have to look like an Iranian now that you are in Iran." Zia and I got so excited to wear veils that needed no knots. Everyone seemed happy but Baba. He looked at Razeq, Naser, Khaleq, and Zaher, and they all were wearing blue jeans. "How ugly," Baba said with his head down, knowing that soon he was going to look like them; he had to.

Instead of taking off his baggy Afghan *tumbans*, he put the jeans over them, tucked in his long Afghan *perahan*, which was longer than the shirt Qasem gave him. Baba wore a black long-sleeved shirt and a suit jacket over it. He looked so different.

"Baba, I like the shape of your ass," Razeq said. "It's my first time seeing it!" The whole room filled with laughter. It had been a long time since we laughed all together.

Qasem didn't want us to sit somewhere we could be seen, so he told everyone to find a spot in the back of the truck, which was nicer than the one from the night before. It even had a top. I found my usual place on Nana's lap and fell asleep.

When I woke up, everyone besides Baba was asleep. "Baba, why are you crying?" I asked him, but he smiled at me and said, "I am not crying, my eyes just aren't working as well as yours." After a few more tears dropped from Baba's eyes, he cleaned his cheeks and stared at the small hole in the roof of the truck that allowed the light to come in.

"Can you tell me what time it is?" he asked. Baba gave me his watch but wasn't surprised when I told him that I couldn't read time.

He pointed to the watch. "There are three arrows inside the watch, one is the tallest one, which keeps moving. Can you see it?" I told him yes. "That counts seconds, one, two, three. When it gets to sixty, meaning it has passed the number twelve, it opens the way for the minute hand to move a step forward," he said. "Then it is the time for the minute hand to give back. Once it passes twelve, it helps the hour hand to move one step forward. It is a teamwork; they all work together to bring nights and days."

If Baba's God and poverty did not always require so much time from Baba, then he probably would have known I couldn't read time, and I would have known that he was fun to spend time with.

The day that we were all locked in the back of the dirty, cold truck was a beautiful day for me: Baba and I got to know each other. He told me a story that I would never forget:

> Once upon a time, there was the Sun; humans called her pure gold. She had everything, but she was still sad. Then one day she decided to go on a walk around the sky. As she was strolling, she felt a little chilly. *What a wonderful, unique experience*, she thought. Miss Sun walked a few more steps and then she peeked to see what was hidden on the other side of the earth that had given her the chills, and she saw Mr. Moon. Her eyes turned brighter; she felt even hotter.
>
> The heat reached Mr. Moon. "Where is this wonderful warmth coming from?" asked cold Mr. Moon. Miss Sun, who was so shy, revealed herself to Mr. Moon. "*Khoday man*, my dear god, you are so warm," said Mr. Moon to Miss Sun. "And you are so cool," Miss Sun responded, as her closed lips struggled to stretch to form a smile.

Suddenly she screamed, "Oh no!" and put her fiery hands on her mouth. "Don't be afraid, it's just a smile! You are happy, and I have it too. Look!"

In just a glance, they were in love. They loved how different they were, there was so much to explore. Their first gift to each other was a smile.

They wanted to give each other more love, so they quit expressing themselves from afar and took a few steps closer. Mr. Moon began to sweat and Miss Sun began to shiver as they got closer. Soon the smiles on their faces faded away. Miss Sun's heat burned Mr. Moon, and Mr. Moon's cold temperature hurt Miss Sun. But nothing stopped them, not even their differences, from crossing the sky to hug each other. They hugged and their hearts were filled with joy, but their eyes cried from the pain of extreme heat and cold.

Mr. Moon's tears dropped on the earth and turned into massive oceans, and Miss Sun's tears turned into millions of shiny stars in the sky. After that day, Mr. Moon was never alone at night because he lived in the heart of stars that hugged him so tightly. And Miss Sun never felt alone during the days because she saw her reflection in the oceans and felt the coolness of Mr. Moon whenever she came out.

By the time Baba finished his story, everyone was awake, listening with so much joy.

With that story, Baba filled my head with hope, my cold face with a smile, and my eyes with a vision that nothing was impossible. "I love you, Baba," I said in my head since I was too shy to say such a thing, and it wasn't something we said to each other.

I had been hoping to arrive a little later at our destination so I could hear more stories, when Qasem stopped the truck and said, "We are in Mashhad, do you see the city?" There was nothing around us besides flat lands colored white. "I have to drop you off here to go check the last checkpoint and make sure my friend who is going to get us across is there." We watched him until he disappeared down the long white road.

There was nothing—not even a tree to shelter us from the snowflakes landing on our faces, hands, and feet. I looked at the gray sky; the fog from my mouth looked like a thick cloud. Miss Sun, hurry up, come, I need you, Baba needs you, we need your warmth! I saw a car approaching us from far away. Razeq took his hands from his pockets and began to wave until the car stopped.

The driver rolled down the window and asked, "How did you end up here, where are you going?"

Nana said, "To the city, Mashhad," as she pointed to the horizon.

The driver laughed and asked, "Are you Afghani?"

"Yes," said Nana.

"That is why you don't know where Mashhad is. Where you are pointing is just a small town; Mashhad is far away!" said the driver. "With a car it might take two or three days in this weather." Nana began to tear up. I felt so angry at Qasem for lying to us.

"We have enough money to pay you; we're freezing to death, can you take us to the town?" Razeq repeated his question a few times until the driver understood.

"I can take only five of you," he said.

"We can even sit in the trunk," said Razeq.

"I already have stuff in the trunk," he said, and drove away.

Razeq tried to convince Nana and Baba to leave, but they wouldn't. As the car got farther away, Nana began to cry louder, as if that was our only ticket to survive.

"We can follow the road, it will end somewhere," said Razeq. We walked and walked, and wished to see any animals but the scariest and most cruel one, humans.

We ate the last pieces of bread but still felt hungry, and wore the last pieces of clothing but still felt cold. I shivered and cried from pain, and poor Baba couldn't even open his eyes anymore. I held his hand and told him to keep his eyes closed. "How could he do that?" Nana repeated to herself.

Suddenly in the middle of nowhere, we heard the call for prayer, "Allah Akbar, Allah Akbar . . . God is great, God is great." We all stopped walking and looked around for the mosque. "It's coming from there," I pointed to the right, where a small light was burning bright enough to show us the way.

"Allah Akbar, Allah Akbar." Baba smiled and recited alongside the prayer coming from the mosque. As we got closer, the little light revealed the beautiful mosque. There were no footprints in the snow; it was only us, I thought.

Razeq opened the door, and we rushed inside where an old man Baba's age was seated on a carpet praying. Baba let go of my hand and sat on the carpet, next to the old man, and began to pray. He looked so happy, he prayed and shivered. It didn't matter how cold he was, he felt warm to reunite with God again.

We put all of our belongings by the door and rushed to the

woodstove. As the heat sat on my cold skin, I felt burning. It took a long time for my body to adjust to the room temperature. "Who are you? Who let you in?" the old man asked Baba angrily.

"We heard the prayer. Isn't this a mosque?" asked Baba in a calm voice.

"Illegal Afghanis! You smell! Out, now!" Just a few seconds ago, while the old man was praying, he looked like a calm and kind person, but he turned into a monster. "You smell bad. This is God's house; leave now or I will call the police."

"It's so cold outside, have mercy on my father and my little sister," said Razeq. The old man said no more and walked to the next room. We all sat down near the fire. But then we heard, "Hello, police?" At that moment, we all ran toward the door and left the mosque without even having time to tie our shoes.

"Wherever you hide, your footsteps will show the police the way you went. There is nowhere to go," yelled the old man and closed the door as we ran in the thick snow.

We found our way on the main road again. The wheels of cars passing by had melted the snow, which made walking easier. Baba and Razeq were in the back, and I was running in front of everyone else, who had slowed down because they were carrying our belongings. I wished Mr. Moon could darken everywhere so we could hide in the darkness. I stopped in my spot to take a break when I saw a car with blue and red lights approaching us from afar.

We slid down the hill on the side of the road and hid under a bridge. We saw the car passing over our heads when the blue and red lights reflected on the snow. I took off my wet shoe that had a small hole in it and put my big toe in my mouth. It felt like an ice cube. Latif began to weep from hearing Baba trying to convince us to leave him there and run before the police could find us. “I didn’t drag you on my back on the tallest mountains to leave you here, Baba,” said Razeq as his teeth chattered. Once Razeq soothed Baba, he, Naser, and Khaleq built big snowballs that blocked the cold wind.

“We have to walk; I see no cars here or by the mosque,” said Razeq. Mr. Moon was still in the sky in a peaceful sleep, but we needed it to be dark everywhere to continue our secret journey. We climbed the slippery hill and began to run, taking a break only when I had to pee.

Baba looked a little better. He put a small blanket around me and continued walking. I was falling asleep when Naser excitedly told us to look at the horizon. Seeing its lights from afar, I wished for one thing: to meet people who could be a little kind to us. We had come a long way, our souls were so fragile, and our bodies were so weak.

As we passed by the first house in the town, I wanted to cry from happiness because we were all alive. The moment we arrived in the heart of the city, I saw the most beautiful thing: a school, with flowers, butterflies, and apple trees on the walls; it was probably where Ranjita had learned to draw. The town was covered with snow, but it still looked full of life. We saw people walking by, cars unloading fruit, and a bread shop on the other side of the street.

There was so much to look at, but I was still watching the girls with their school uniforms and colorful backpacks. Some of them were with their parents, some were alone. They watched us too, probably wondering why we didn’t have an umbrella. I wished I could tell them we had no home, or that we had walked hundreds of miles to find a home where they were. There was so much I could share with them. Once the last girl made her way to the school, the doors closed and I heard the girls singing a song together.

"They are Afghani," I heard one of the passersby say, referring to us. Like the old man in the mosque, he sounded disgusted.

How bad is being an Afghan? I asked myself. The people looking at us had two hands and two legs, and so did we, but they still reacted to seeing an Afghan as if they had seen a monster.

We had no idea what was next; our main plan was to find a way to get some bread. I had seen people walking with bread in their hands; I wanted to smell it and eat it warm, and if possible, drink sweet green tea with it. The bread shop was a few steps away from us. The fear of trying to speak the Iranian language stopped Razeq from trying to purchase some bread.

"I can speak some Persian," I said. I wasn't sure of my decision, but I was so desperate; I wanted some bread. Nana took out some Iranian money, unsure what each bill was worth, and she gave me one. Razeq helped me cross the street and waited outside the bread shop. I stood in line, and a man in line saw me shivering and let me go next. "Bread," I said, only one word, and gave the shop owner the money.

"How many?" he asked. I counted all the days we had not eaten and said, "Twenty." He smiled and said, "You can only get seven, but I will give you ten—three for your family as a welcome gift." He was so kind; he made me feel hopeful.

The moment I held the warm bread, I felt alive. I couldn't wait to eat again. We all got a whole fresh warm piece of bread, savoring it as snow fell on our faces and our belongings. We were done eating when a guy from the line came up to us with bread in his hands.

"Like you, I walked hundreds of miles, passing the mountains where I lost my sister," he said. His words brought him to tears, as he gave us the pile of bread.

Baba stood up to hug the man, saying, "Brother, you speak our language." He was a little younger than Baba with a nice hat, a long cream-colored coat, and warm leather boots.

"I am from Herat too," the man said. "The war has scattered all of us like seeds. My oldest sister is in Turkey, and my brothers are in America. Do you know where Turkey and America are?"

"So far we know only about Afghanistan, India, and Iran—are there more countries?" asked Razeq. The man looked at all of us and told us that there are many more countries that we haven't even seen pictures of.

"Where is your destination?" the man asked.

"Mashhad," said Nana. The man stood up, made a phone call, and then returned to us. People stared at us when they saw us seated in the snow having a conversation while the color returned to our faces. Baba looked alive again. We all felt and looked better to see an Afghan and to no longer have to hide our identities.

"On my way," said the man on the phone. He helped Baba get up and asked us to follow him. Once we turned onto the deserted road, I saw a big bus by the road. The Herati man shook the driver's hand and said, "He is one of my best and most trusted drivers. I have a transportation company, and Jalil has been with me since the start of it. He will get you to Mashhad."

Baba tried to kiss the man's hand, but the man kissed Baba's hand instead, telling him that doing this for us made him feel so much better. Jalil opened the bus luggage compartment and put a blanket inside. "It will be warm enough once we put in more suitcases," he said, "and the moment we pass the police checkpoint, I will have seats for you."

The Herati man hugged Baba and said goodbye. I looked in the luggage compartment: it looked comfortable. Jalil closed the door, and it got so dark inside. I closed my eyes to rest since in the darkness there was nothing to see. As the bus moved, we held our hands tight and hoped to be in Mashhad when we woke up.

I could have slept in the luggage compartment for days if Jalil had not opened the door to let the light and the cold in. "You're safe now, and I have seats for you," he said. I stepped outside. Instead of gas lamps, I saw tall streetlights; instead of muddy streets, I saw asphalt; and instead of clay walls with bullet holes, I saw smooth mosaic façades holding up tall buildings around an empty parking lot.

No one was on the street; everyone had a home. Only God saw the illegal Afghans, us, making it to the end of the road that carried unbearable pain. We had made it. Now we were on the road to take us home; we were going to have a home too.

"You can sit wherever you like," said Jalil, as he put on his seatbelt. The moment I entered the bus, I experienced the wonderful feeling of warmth. I took one of the many empty seats and felt alive again. "Where in Mashhad are you going?" asked Jalil.

"We're not sure," Nana told him. "But we heard Ali Timur is where some Afghans live." Nana told Jalil the name of the neighborhood where Ranjita's mother used to live.

"Oh, sure you will find Afghans there. I know where it is; I'll take you there," said Jalil and slowly left the parking lot.

Jalil was playing some music. "I love her voice. Who is she?" Razeq asked him.

"Her name is Hayedeh, my favorite artist," Jalil said. "Do you have a favorite artist?"

"I do," Razeq said. "Ahmad Zahir."

"Oh, I know him!"

That put a big smile on Razeq's face. "Is singing *haram* here too?" he asked.

"Not for men, especially if you sing about God and Muhammad," said Jalil.

I put my head against the cold window and wished I could stop blinking. I didn't want to miss seeing the beautiful tall buildings, cars on the road, banners, stores, street signs.

"*Khodaya!*" No one said anything besides "Wow!"—as if we had all forgotten how to speak when we saw the golden dome of the Imam Reza shrine winking at us from afar.

On the way, we saw girls my age with pink school uniforms and white veils. How fun! As we crossed the busy street, I understood that all the stories we had heard about girls going to school in Iran were true. I stopped watching the beautiful city only when my eyes involuntarily closed and I slept, with my head leaning against the window. I slept so well. I felt rested, warm, hungry, and excited for the darkness of the night slowly lifting.

When we got to our destination, Jalil parked the bus and told us, "You are here. I would help you find a *banga* [rental agency] to rent a house, but I must leave for my next destination."

"I wish I had more than my prayers to give you and thank you for saving us," said Nana.

Jalil smiled and said, "You know who to thank, Mother."

"May God be with you," said Baba, and we watched the big bus disappear down the road.

Left to right: Latif; my brother's baby, Naser; and Baba after our arrival in Mashhad.

8

Ms. Zahra and Her Daughters

We knew that we needed to find a home, but where? How? Nana repeated the sentence Jalil had taught us, "*Yeh khune mikhayem, Agha* [We need a house, sir]," over and over, to make it sound more like an Iranian. It didn't matter how many times she practiced it, the first *banga* man guessed our true identity and told us to leave.

Nana told him that we had money. "But you have no permission to be in Iran, so go before I'm in trouble," he said.

We checked the fourth and fifth *banga*; they all found a reason to say no to us. "You are illegal, you don't have enough money to rent a two-bedroom house, you are a big family," said another man.

Nana and I returned to our temporary shelter, the bus station, and waited until Razeq and Naser returned. "Nothing!" said Razeq.

Hunger followed exhaustion, stopping everyone from looking for a *banga*. There was a grocery store a few steps away from us, but we were too scared to face its owner. "Kokosto, go and get us food," said Razeq, putting Iranian money inside my pocket.

"Speak less, and know that I will be watching out for you,"

said Nana. She and Baba thought I was too young to be deported, but I was too young to face such a scary moment too. I tried to argue, but soon I was putting my foot inside the store, feeling weak and scared.

"What do you want, little one?" a lady with a black veil said to me. She approached me from the end of the store. I still felt scared and unsafe even though she had a smile on her face. Would it still be there once she knew I was an Afghan?

"I want this, this too, and this, and those," I said, pointing. I filled up the black plastic bag with whatever looked delicious in the picture on the package. I gave her the money with a rubber band around it. She gave me the extra money back and said goodbye, still smiling.

We began the search for a home again, but this time with a new plan: lying. Nana sold all the valuable jewelry we had taken from the Taliban and made her way to the *banga* man who had rejected Naser and Razeq earlier. The moment we entered the *banga*, I saw the most interesting thing in my life: a color TV mounted on a white wall covered with pictures of the Kaaba, and on the TV I saw drawings of a cat and mouse, but they moved! They were alive!

After saying salaam, Nana began her lies: "Yes, it is only me, my two daughters, and two sons."

"Is she your youngest child?" The *banga* man pointed at me.

"Yes." Nana told the truth, the only truth since her conversation began. "Say salaam, Sonita," said Nana, disappointed in me for not being able to take my eyes off the TV and laughing out loud each time the mouse came up with clever, funny tricks to stop the cat from eating him.

"Every child wakes up early in the morning to see this, even me sometimes," said the *banga* man with a laugh. Then he picked up the conversation where he had left it. "Do you want to see the house first?"

"Does the house have water?" Nana asked.

"Yes."

"Does it have a common room?"

"Yes," repeated the *banga* man.

"It sounds like a dream house, no need to visit it."

The *banga* man laughed. "This is very interesting. So you have an ID or an Iranian witness?"

"No ID, no witness."

"Sorry, Mother," said the man. "I can't help you without an ID or an Iranian guarantor."

"We have nowhere to go," Nana said with sorrow. "Soon people will kick us out of the bus station too. We're so tired, we have no shelter." She kept crying and begging the *banga* man to give us a place, even for just the night, until we found somewhere to live.

"I think I know a place where you could live," he said. "Follow me." From a dozen keys, he picked one and led the way. We walked a few blocks away from the *banga*, passed all the nice houses, and stopped by a small, gray, rusted door. "You can live here, if you can pay the rent I mentioned," he said, and showed Nana around. "Sorry, it doesn't look like a dream house: the countertop in the kitchen is broken, the bathroom window is also broken. I was planning to renovate this place, but it seems like you really need a place, so this is what is available," said the *banga* man.

The house looked nothing like what we had seen in Afghanistan: a big common room with a kitchen in the right corner, a shower in the left corner, and a big guest room to the right of the kitchen. The walls and the floor were not made of clay; they were concrete. There was no need to burn wood to cook or keep the house warm; there was gas in the kitchen and common room. There was no need to carry buckets of water from a well; water was available in the kitchen, in the shower, even in the bathroom—rotating the faucet handles, we could get cold and hot water. How wasn't this a dream house?

"This is more than what we could have asked for; may God grant you your biggest wishes," said Nana to the *banga* man.

They finalized the agreement, which required Nana's fingerprint and a few months of rent. We found our way back to the family, and everyone's eyes brightened when Nana showed them the paper. We stood up, took our belongings, and left the bus station.

Latif was impatient to know where we were headed. "What does it look like?" When we reached the house, everyone kept quiet until we were inside and the front door was closed. When I turned on the light, Latif's jaw dropped, and she said, "*Khoday man*! [oh my god]" She was so amazed that she no longer had to deal with gas lamps. Suddenly the empty house filled with joy, laughter, and smiles. Nana was right: the end of every stormy night is a sunny day.

"*Afghani kasif*!" When the kids in our new neighborhood first called me that, I rushed to our house, took a long shower, brushed my hair, and then went back outside. But no matter how hard I tried, they still called me a dirty Afghani, even when I smelled and looked cleaner than most of them.

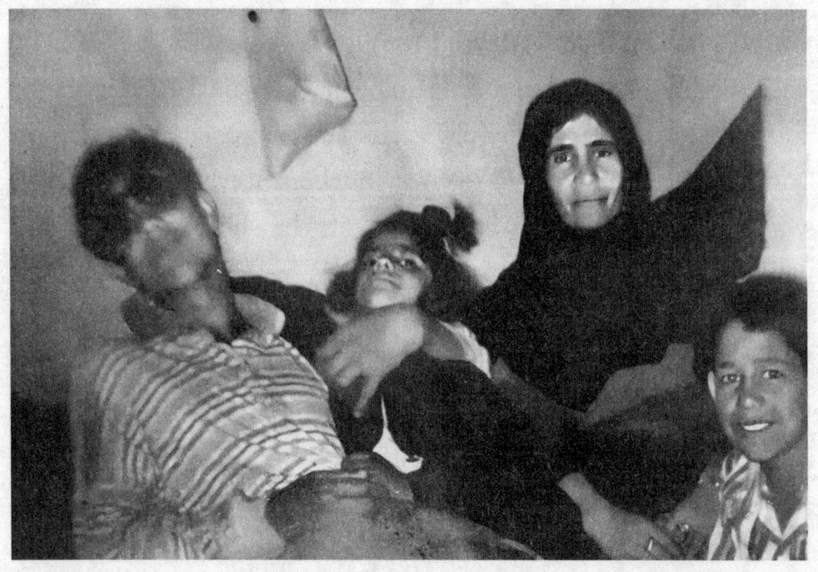

Left to right: Razeq, me, Nana, and Zaher. Our new life in Iran.

As I walked home feeling lonely, I pondered over and over, thinking of Ranjita. Did people call her by the same name? How much did she miss the days when people used to call her by her own name? Well, I did. In just a few days I became homesick; I even missed the Akhund because he called me by my name. And I missed Shir Khan because he included me in a few games if not all. I missed being seen.

But among all those people who tried not to see us, there was a kind lady, Ms. Zahra, who lived near us. She met Nana and me in a line when we were buying naan. Nana learned a lot from Ms. Zahra, who told us her name without any fear.

"My name is Keshwar," said Nana.

"Wow, so your name means a country?"

"Yes," said Nana. Although Ms. Zahra liked Nana's name, Nana changed her name to Fatemeh, a name we heard in Iran over and over. Baba and Nana also changed our last name from

Payandeh to Alizadeh, which sounded more fitting in an Iranian community. We all thought our last name could help us face less discrimination, but no one really cared.

Latif often joined Ms. Zahra and her two daughters, Monireh and Hamideh, to watch soccer, which was very boring to me. Latif began to like soccer and had crushes on about five or six of the players, who were tall and had nice hair.

I loved their big color TV. One day I went to get ice from Ms. Zahra, planning to watch TV, but she sent me home right away to tell Baba and Nana: "Afghanistan is free!" I was confused until our whole family returned to Ms. Zahra's house. She hugged Nana and said, "Afghanistan is free of the Taliban!" Would this mean we could return home, to Aziz, to the Karbar, to Ranjita?

I thought I would never see the faces of the Taliban again, but there they were on the TV screen. "Those are American soldiers," Ms. Zahra told Razeq.

Baba smiled and thanked God several times. Razeq was in shock: How could America defeat the most powerful group we all knew? We had heard the name "America" on our way to Iran—where was it? I wondered how far it was from Iran.

Everyone was so happy that no one went to work. Instead, my family spent more money than usual and invited Ms. Zahra and her daughters for a feast. After that, we became one family that lived in two different houses, as Nana said.

Because of Ms. Zahra, Nana or Baba had no problem when Zia wanted to play outside. They even let Latif go to Ms. Zahra's house without a chaperone to visit her daughters. The daughters were so free—Hamideh even had the freedom to go to school. She became a role model for me and Zia, if not everyone.

One day I asked Ms. Zahra's daughters, "How do you write 'Sonita'?" Then everyone else became interested in learning how to write their names.

We were truly like a family. Ms. Zahra even helped my brothers find jobs that were less risky for undocumented refugees. Soon Razeq and Naser became *namakis*, people who look in garbage cans for plastic, papers, and whatever could be sold. Zaher and Khaleq started to shine shoes. I knew that we were financially stable when our breakfast shifted from sweet tea with bread to sweet tea with bread *and* eggs.

Ms. Zahra even found a job for Nana, Latif, Zia, and me to make Muharram chains for her. We joined many other women seated in rows in Ms. Zahra's big yard. One was an Afghan woman who had fled to Iran before us. Her daughters and little son could speak with an Iranian accent very well. Nana and the Afghan woman, Zamarod, began to talk about how difficult the journey to come to Iran was. Ms. Zahra had heard the tale before, but she still listened while we all made chains.

Ms. Zahra gave us a bucket with tools. "Your job is to put these loops together to make a chain this size." She showed us several examples to make sure we understood. I wasn't sure why Ms. Zahra needed thousands of little chains until one day I saw an Iranian film. In one scene, the character joined the Muharram ceremony and almost everyone had in their hands a little chain like Ms. Zahra's. They used the chain to hit themselves on their shoulders and repeated the name of the prophet Husain to wash away their sins.

I liked the idea of washing away our sins by hitting ourselves, so the next day, Zia and I took the chains we made and began to hit ourselves on our backs. We never took the task seriously, and Ms. Zahra let us play.

Ms. Zahra's kindness made me so bold. After work, Zia and I played hopscotch, even when bullies were present on our street. Wandering around the neighborhood, markets, and schools nearby was our daily routine for a long time, until Baba became ill and had to be hospitalized. The costs were so high that no one in the family could afford to be without a job, and extra help from us was needed.

When Muharram was over, Ms. Zahra brought apricot nuts home for us to break and separate the seeds from the broken shells. Then I was given a new assignment—to shine shoes with Zaher.

Learning how to find customers and begging people to shine their shoes: it reminded me of the days I begged for bread, but begging for a piece of bread was easier. Zaher often wanted me to do the begging because people felt bad sending someone so young back empty-handed. I'd mastered my job by then and was sent to work alone, but Zaher and Khaleq were always nearby.

"Oh hello," said a big guy to me as he took off his shoes. "I was expecting you today, my shoes look dusty without you." He used to be Zaher's permanent customer and now was mine. He introduced me to a little girl in a pink and white school uniform.

I was supposed to focus on my job, but I was a little distracted. Her backpack was just like mine but cleaner because she carried books, and I carried shoe polish. I quickly brushed the dust off the big guy's shoes and put on more shoe polish than usual. I snuck a look at the girl, who was living my dream. Work and exhaustion had made me forget that I had a dream to learn how to read and write. Seeing her reminded me. That day, once I made enough money, I ran back to where Zia and I had seen school uniforms.

I had never shopped for clothing before. *How should I start the conversation*? I asked myself. So I pointed to a uniform and said, "Can I have that?" The man helping me at first insisted that I bring my mother with me because I didn't know my size. But eventually, he let me try on different sizes until I found one that fit. I didn't want to take the clothes off, so I gave him the money and left the market. With the uniform on, I felt so great—so close to my dream.

"Did you spend money on that?" Nana said when she saw me in the uniform. She screamed at me for wasting money and probably would have punished me if Ms. Zahra's daughter hadn't been there to defend me. I knew she would punish me if I told her that I was going to go to school. After all, Nana thought school was a waste of time and money. So, I kept quiet and shared my plan only with Zia.

In the morning, to Nana's surprise, I was too happy to leave the house to "work." I saw a few girls in pink, so I followed them. Although my backpack was in such poor condition, the rest of me looked all new. I had the same white veil and pink uniform as the girls. Each step I took filled my chest with more anxiety and hope. When I got closer to the school, I ran past the watchman and made it inside the courtyard. I stood in the middle of a big hall, watching the girls go inside one of the rooms.

"Where is your class?" the watchman asked me.

"I don't know," I said. "I want to learn how to read and write."

"Are you Afghani?"

"Yes."

"You need to find another school," he said, walking me outside. He closed the door, saying, "Afghanis aren't allowed here."

There I was, thinking that all I needed to do was to look like them, to wear a uniform, but they wanted me to change my identity. How could I do that? I would, if they would show me how. Feeling heartbroken, I sat a few steps away from the school and continued to watch it.

I no longer felt good in the uniform I had dreamed of having. I was about to leave to go to work when a lady with a long black hijab asked if I was lost. When I told her the reason I was seated alone and crying, she sat next to me and began to talk quietly. "I'm a teacher," she told me. My heart instantly felt less broken.

She asked me to walk with her, and without any second thought, I followed her. In just a few minutes, we arrived at a mosque. She took me to the back of the mosque, where there was a room where women prayed. "What is your name?" she asked.

"Sonita," I said.

"How old are you?"

"I don't know," I responded.

"Sonita, this will be your school and class from now on," the woman said, "but it is a secret class. You shouldn't tell anyone, okay?"

"Okay."

"We meet every other day," she said. "Do you have a notebook?" When I told her I didn't, she said, "I will get a book and a notebook for you."

"Can my sister come too?" I asked.

"Sure!"

When I heard that, I felt joy and happiness.

9

A Student at Last

When I told Latif about what had happened, she said that I shouldn't trust a stranger. But the next day I wore my uniform and organized my work backpack to leave room for the notebook and the book the woman had promised me. I left the house around the time my brothers left to go to work. Nana was at the hospital taking care of Baba, which meant that Zia could come with me.

Though we left full of energy like the early morning birds, our spirits dropped when we entered the mosque. I saw dozens of shoes outside, all for adults. Zia and I entered the main door to walk through the big room where men were busy praying. I opened the door that the Lady said led to our classroom, interrupting many women praying. There was no room for me or Zia, but we walked to the corner of the room and began to search for her.

Was it all a lie? I looked around but found no sign of school there. Zia and I decided we should leave the room, but we were too scared to walk among the angry women, who reminded me of the Akhund. They all moved back and forth reciting the same thing.

After a short time, the Lady came inside. I felt so happy to see her. She acted as if she didn't know me until the last woman in the room left. "Salaam, so happy to see you. What was your name again?" she asked.

I reminded her of my name and Zia's. Soon more kids younger and older than us joined. Instead of sitting down to receive lessons, they each took a broom and cleaning towels and walked down the hall where the men were. They said nothing to the Lady besides greeting her: "Hello, Teacher."

"Here is one thing to know before we start," she said once the place was cleared of men and women. "In order to have this place available for us to learn, we must clean it every other day." She instructed Zia and me to help with taking care of the trash cans.

It was so fun to be among many other children from Afghanistan; we played as we cleaned. Then we all found a place to sit in the small room with a big window facing the street. The Lady put down the curtain, checked the hall and the yard, and asked us to sit down. It reminded me of the nights we used to go to Uncle Ghani's house to watch TV and had to cover all the windows. About ten students sat on the floor in two rows back-to-back and waited for instructions from the Lady.

"Bring out your religious books," said the Lady, and gave Zia and me a book to share. I felt so unhappy; it felt like it was going to be the same as at Masjid Safid. I wanted to learn how to read and write—not to memorize things! Soon she made it clear that the religious books were there to pretend that we were learning the Quran, not reading and writing, as it was illegal for undocumented Afghans to learn and for Iranians to teach them.

"If we ever have a visitor, we put our notebooks and non-religious books away and open up our religious books—you got it?" she asked Zia and me. After we accepted all the rules, she gave us notebooks, two pencils, and two books. Zia and I flipped through the pages full of color and pictures.

Once all the assignments were done and the Lady had checked each one, she asked Zia and me to stand up and introduce ourselves. After we shared our names, she said, "Now tell us what you want to be in the future. Or, what is your biggest dream?"

"I don't know," I said. I reminded myself of the definition of "dream" from the conversations I had heard and stories I had been told—"dream" meant wanting something that was unachievable.

"My dream is to learn to read and write," Zia said.

"Wonderful! I guess you are going in the right direction," the Lady replied and asked me to share mine.

"I want to read and write too." I repeated what Zia had said, but it was true.

The Lady asked us to sit down and pay attention to how she introduced herself. "Hello, my name is Ms. Rahmati, I am forty-six years old, and my biggest dream is to teach refugee children to go to college and become change-makers," she said and sat down. "Now you, Sonita, introduce yourself with your chin up and speak up!"

"Hello, my name is Sonita. I am . . ." I looked at Zia for help, but she didn't know how old she was, either. "Let's assume you are six years old," said Ms. Rahmati.

"Hello, my name is Sonita, I am six years old, and my dream is to be able to read and write," I said.

"Wonderful! Now you, Zia." Once Zia also passed the first lesson, our "introductions," Ms. Rahmati closed the rusty iron door and began to write something in chalk on the back of it. "Okay, we review before our new lesson," she said, as she pointed her stick toward the words: "Water, Bread, Father. Water, Bread, Father." We repeated the words together, and most students had confidence that what they were saying was correct. I couldn't wait to be one of them, to name whatever Ms. Rahmati pointed at.

Once she was sure that we could not recognize any of the words she pointed at, she gave us letters to write. "Aleph, Beh, Peh, repeat after me," said Ms. Rahmati. Zia and I repeated. She was happy to know that we knew the letters in order, but we couldn't recognize them in written form. She gave Zia and me a few letters to write and repeat after writing them. Once our assignment was over, she asked everyone to take a break.

All the children ran to the yard to play. Those who had a snack ate, and those who did not watched. Zia and I watched. We had no idea the class would have a break time; otherwise, we could have brought some bread or leftovers.

"Would you like some *ghormeh sabzi*?" Ms. Rahmati asked. I didn't know what *ghormeh sabzi* was, but her food smelled so good! I was too shy to say yes, but she left some for me and Zia. It was rice and something with beans and meat. I put a spoonful of food in my mouth and—MY GOD! SO GOOD! Zia had more than me since I couldn't chew faster.

"*Ghormeh sabzi, ghormeh sabzi.*" I repeated the name a few times to remember it, in case someone might ask me what my favorite food was. Once our stomachs were full, Zia and I joined a game, *wasat tanha*, similar to the one that the kids in our neighborhood played.

For the first time I liked being in a mosque, but class was over and work had to start. As I shined shoes, I repeated, "Aleph, Beh, Peh . . ." They were the same as the letters in the Siparah, but the pencil and the notebook made it so much more exciting. I wanted to read what was written on the doors of each store I entered to shine shoes, on the TV ads, on the water bills that we often had to take to Ms. Zahra's daughters to read.

When I got home, Baba was back from the hospital. I was happy to see him. "Take a shower before the smell of your feet makes us unconscious," said Latif as she prepared the table. I was still in such a wonderful mood that I couldn't wait to share about my day of going to school for the first time. "Baba, Nana, Zia and I went to school today," I said with so much excitement.

"We heard that already," said Nana, disapproving of the extra cost of time and money on pencils and notebooks. When Zia told them that we got everything for free, then they said nothing and continued to eat.

"I will be able to read and write all your names," I said.

The next day I asked to take off a day from work so I could play with Zia. Nana agreed, but said first Zia had to help with separating apricot seeds from shells. I had to play all by myself, I thought.

But Baba, who couldn't walk much, made his way to the entrance door and sat on the small carpet I had put outside our house. He took his small radio from his pocket and began to search for any channels that offered news about Afghanistan. Once he found a news channel, he put the small radio near his ear, but he couldn't hear much so gave up and put his radio away.

"What are you looking at?" Baba asked. I showed him my favorite pages in the book. "I can't see well, it's all blurry," he said, so I described the page to Baba. He liked it. He took it from me and put it closer to his eyes.

I asked him if he wished to go to school with me, and he said that he had already finished the Quran and didn't know that there were more books out there than the Quran. The Quran was good to learn to recite, but my book was supposed to help me speak my mind, as my teacher said. "I want to go to school and become a doctor," I told him, saying the sentence I had learned from Ms. Zahra's daughter.

"Ha-ha! Make sure to become an eye doctor, so you can help me to see you again," said Baba, as he scanned the channels on his radio.

10

Jabbar

Days went by quickly, as Zia and I had school to keep us busy, and Latif had her new friends, Tazehgul and Anis, Zamarod's daughters. Though Latif often hung out with Ms. Zahra's daughters, she had more fun and laughter when she spent time with Zamarod's daughters. They spoke our language and knew many of the references Latif made. I loved hanging out at Zamarod's house. They had a big farm filled with flowers and grapevines.

One day, Zia and I were at their house while everyone was busy cooking for the big lunch gathering they had. Zia and I began to collect bunches of flowers until Latif stopped us and cursed at us quietly in the far corner of the house where Zamarod and her husband couldn't hear. When we quit bringing shame to Latif by misbehaving, Zia and I got to work in the kitchen, where stealing food became more fun than picking flowers. Zia, Zamarod's little boys, and I giggled quietly whenever we succeeded in grabbing fried potatoes.

Once the food was ready, someone knocked on the door—the guest that Zamarod was expecting. A tall man with a mustache and black hair came into the living room. He was more beautiful than the main characters of the films that Latif fell in love with.

Zamarod welcomed him, and he looked around to find a safe spot for his motorcycle helmet.

"This is Latif, our neighbor who I told you about," Zamarod said, and the tall man, who was introduced as her brother Jabbar, smiled at Latif. Latif looked at him as she had looked at the *shiryakh* guy back in Afghanistan, and as we all sat around the tablecloth to eat, Jabbar and Latif kept looking at each other. "Latif is a wonderful cook, Jabbar," said Zamarod. Then Jabbar began to comment on each dish he ate. Although he liked them all, he ate less than me; maybe, like Latif, he couldn't eat when he was overwhelmed with happiness.

After lunch, Latif helped Tazehgul prepare tea, and Zamarod played a cassette and asked all the children, including Zia and me, to sit down to open the floor for Jabbar. He didn't really need to dance to gain Latif's attention; he had it the moment he showed up. Disregarding everyone else in the room, Zamarod asked Latif to dance on the same dance floor that Jabbar was dancing on.

It looked like the Bollywood movies where the guy and the girl dance together—only a tree and rain were missing; the rest was exactly the same.

It took Latif a while to say goodbye to everyone. She wanted to stay longer, but she had to rush home before my brothers arrived. Zamarod told Zia and me not to speak to anyone about Jabbar or dancing.

Soon after Latif met Jabbar, she asked Zia and me to be her teachers. "How do you write *dooset daram*?" she asked. We didn't yet know how to write sentences such as "I love you," so Latif decided to take lessons with Ms. Zahra's daughter, who could teach her more sophisticated things.

By then, Zia and I had learned how to write "Weather,

Father, Rain," and a few other words but couldn't make a sentence with them. Whenever I saw one of the words I had learned from TV ads, billboards, and other places, I would proudly point to it and tell my family, "I know that word!"

Latif wanted to fast-forward through the basics and learn how to write love letters like the ones Jabbar put together for her, either by himself or with the help of someone. Latif bragged about "Literate Jabbar," joking with Ms. Zahra's daughters, "I would never learn anything from him since his eyes are too distracting, ha-ha!"

One day, when I got home from work, I saw flowers on the kitchen counter. A voice coming from the guest room was congratulating Latif on her engagement. Nana, Baba, Ms. Zahra, and her daughters were all there drinking tea. Everyone looked so happy, especially Latif, who was seated near the doorway, playing with her cup and smiling at a picture of Jabbar on the carpet in front of her—as if Latif had no idea what he looked like.

"He is a very tall guy, probably the tallest in our family," said Baba, not knowing that was not news to Latif, who had danced with him and stood by his shoulder. Soon my brothers returned from work, and Nana shared the news with them.

"Latif had a suitor come today," said Nana with a smile.

"Did Baba accept it?" Naser asked and was very happy to hear that Baba had accepted the engagement.

"How much is the *pishkash*? And who is he?" Razeq asked. I can't recall Latif's price, but I guess they paid Baba enough that in just a few days we purchased new carpets and a color TV, and I was no longer pushed to work.

Since Latif was engaged, she was allowed to put on makeup and go outside if she wanted. Sometimes Jabbar sent her money to go to a beauty salon. She cut her hair and trimmed her bushy eyebrows—all things that couldn't be done until a girl was engaged. "I want to get married so I can look nice too," I said.

Latif laughed. "You could look nice if you just brushed your hair!" Ms. Zahra's daughters taught her to use makeup since no one in our family had the talent or permission to do so before engagement or marriage. Occasionally, Latif practiced on me or Zia. Sometimes it felt like the three of us were getting married. *How fun to be a bride*, I thought.

Latif never met Jabbar's parents because they were in Afghanistan, Jabbar said. He lived about three hours away from his sister Zamarod and worked in a shoe store.

Once Baba found an Akhund to read passages to make Latif and Jabbar *mahram* (religiously affiliated), Jabbar visited Latif more often and brought more gifts. Sometimes Jabbar wanted to take her on a motorcycle ride. Baba and my brothers wouldn't allow her to go alone, so I would be asked to join them. I loved every part of the ride—until they would stop in the middle of nowhere to kiss.

One day a stranger came to the door and asked me to call my father. When Baba met him outside, he said three or four times, "Jabbar is a drug dealer, don't trust him or his family." He said that we should cancel the marriage, but he never answered who he was or how he knew Jabbar. Baba heard all his words about drugs and violence, and then asked the man to leave and never knock on our door again.

Nana and Baba pondered what he had told them, but Latif defended Jabbar and his family. "I don't even think he smokes cigarettes—how could he be affiliated with drugs?" Baba asked himself and got ready to do his afternoon prayer.

Razeq thought that maybe he or Naser should do a quick

background check on Jabbar, but everyone else figured time would prove Jabbar and his background. It would be such a shame to call the marriage off since Jabbar had held Latif's hand. No one liked to marry second-hand girls; plus, Latif loved him and was happy with him. Slowly we all forgot the day that the stranger visited us, until a night we were all invited to Zamarod's house.

"A few days ago a stranger knocked on our door and accused you of selling drugs," Baba said to Jabbar. Zamarod laughed and said no more.

"Some of my relatives are my biggest enemies and cannot see how successful I am at my job and how I have the ability to form my own family very soon," said Jabbar as he took a spoon of rice in his mouth. He often had a big smile on his face, no matter what happened during the day. Baba liked that and still trusted him, no matter what the stranger had told him.

Every Friday, Jabbar would visit us to have *Namzad bazi* with Latif, holding her hand and hugging her. Since he had paid half of the *pishkash*, he was allowed to be alone with her in a room. "Remember, if he makes you pregnant, your father and brothers will kill you, so nothing except kissing," Nana warned Latif, not knowing that they had already kissed before. In the morning, Latif began cleaning the house, and then focused on herself to look and smell good for Jabbar.

Latif's appearance was changing every day; she was becoming beautiful. She'd struggled a lot until someone asked for her hand. Now she got new clothing, pieces of jewelry, makeup . . . sometimes Jabbar even gave her cash to buy whatever she liked.

That Friday was a special day; it was the New Year celebration, Sezdeh Bedar—thirteen days after the New Year. Early in the morning Razeq played songs and danced around until Jabbar arrived in his big white truck. Baba was interested to know what exactly Jabbar did that allowed him to buy a truck. He often asked Jabbar whether Razeq or Naser could work with him, but Jabbar never responded.

Razeq continued to dance as he got ready. Everyone looked excited and new, just like Eid in Herat. We all were taking the day off to go on a picnic with Jabbar, Zamarod's family, and Ms. Zahra and her two daughters.

Naser put baskets full of food in the back of the truck with a big carpet and told everyone to climb in. "Don't stand up because if a cop stops us, they'll take the truck," said Jabbar and drove away from our street. Ms. Zahra was worried when she learned that Jabbar didn't have a driving certificate, but after a little bit of driving, she trusted him.

On the way we saw people in cars and trucks and on motorcycles, going to celebrate the New Year with their families and friends. On the hood of every car was a plate of fresh grass as a sign of welcoming the new year. At the end of the day, people would tie the grass and wish for wealth, health, or marriage. Latif didn't need to worry about any of those since she seemed to have all of them.

There were hundreds of people on the hills and the mountain where Jabbar parked. "Some of these people had to come here to take a spot before the sun was out," he told us. "We are lucky to find this area on the mountain."

Jabbar was often very scared of holding Latif's hand in public. If the Iranian police stopped them, then he would have to prove that she was legally his fiancée. Then, if he could do that, he had to prove that he was legally in Iran. But today he was with family. "Welcome everyone!" Zamarod and her husband stood up to greet us. Once the carpet was on the ground, everyone found some room to sit down and have a cup of tea.

So much was happening around us—music, games, dancing, clapping, children playing, and kite running. Kite running was a joy we all knew. "Hold it tight!" Razeq told Zia. He had asked her to take the kite to the top of the hill where the wind could take it. Naser and Khaleq's kite was already in the sky, along with dozens of others. None of them looked as cheap and thin as Razeq's and Naser's kites.

While all the other kite runners were satisfied with their kites being in the sky, Razeq took the kite he had made himself and invited Naser for a challenge. They competed to see whose kite could stay in the sky longer and higher. Since I was on Razeq's team, I cheered for him. Suddenly we heard Nana, Zamarod, and Ms. Zahra and her daughters clapping for Naser to win. How funny: we were so lost in the game that we didn't realize we had a bigger audience watching the competition.

Soon we were called for lunch. There was a big tablecloth with about twenty-five people around it. "Well, that was what I called a real kite competition," said Ms. Zahra while putting food on her plate.

"Wow, this is the best kebab I have ever had," Razeq said and thanked Zamarod. She had prepared the food all by herself: rice, chicken korma, lamb, salad, eggplant, and other options. She was such a good cook, I thought maybe one day I could ask her to make me some *ghormeh sabzi*.

Soon Jabbar paid all the money he had promised Baba, which meant Latif's wedding day wasn't far off. One day, Nana, Latif, Zia, and I walked around the marketplace and found nice gold earrings for her. Some brides in Afghanistan would wear fake gold; Latif was lucky to have two real gold rings, a pair of gold earrings, and a fake gold necklace that was indistinguishable from real gold.

After buying the earrings, we made our way to the hair salon where we saw posters of brides. "When I marry, I will have a green wedding dress," I told the group. Latif argued that such a color wouldn't be seen as a real wedding dress because every bride wears white and will continue to wear white.

We went to a second store and then a third, where Latif found the most beautiful dress. The crystal beads around the neck and sleeves shone like the stars of Herat. The veil was long and light, as Latif wished. Latif tried the dress on—and wow! She looked so beautiful, like the models in the windows of the beauty salon. Since the dress was too expensive to buy, she made an arrangement to meet with the shop owner to do her makeup and rent the dress. As we had no ID, the shop owner asked us to come back with an Iranian guarantor to sign on our behalf. Latif didn't worry because Ms. Zahra was there to help.

Next we chose wedding cards, which, like the cards we received in Afghanistan, had a picture of a happy couple on the front of the card. "What is written on it?" Latif asked Zia and me. Zia took the card to give it a try, and I peeked at it to help Zia. "*Mmo, mob, moba, mobar . . .*" Zia and I could recognize all the letters used in the card, but we didn't have enough time to sound every word and make sense of them. So the shop owner told us, "It says: 'We, Mr.________ & Mrs.________ are delighted to invite you to our wedding . . .' "

The day of the wedding was so close that Nana thought that Zia and I had better buy dresses that day. She didn't give us much time to look around, so we picked similar dresses but different shoes. Unlike Zia, I was super excited about our dresses.

Since Zia and I failed our reading test that day, Latif only trusted Ms. Zahra's daughter Monireh to write the wedding cards to the guests. "We, Mr. Jabbar Norzae & Mrs. Norzae are delighted to invite you to our wedding . . ." Monireh filled out the cards, and then Nana put them aside to be delivered to the guests.

Finally, the day to wear my dress arrived. While Latif was in the beauty salon, Zia and I rushed to her makeup bag. Baba was the only one with us, but he couldn't see well, so Zia and I began to put on whatever we could in hopes of making ourselves prettier than Latif and the guests. We started with the white powder, as Latif usually did, then some green eye shadow, red lipstick on our lips, and red lipstick also on our cheeks to make them rosy like the way Latif did. Since Baba wasn't in a rush, Zia and I kept applying more makeup.

When we arrived at Zamarod's house, music was playing and a big couch was in the middle of the hall with a table. On the table were two cups, plates, forks, a big mirror, and the Quran. In a short time, dozens of men, women, and children arrived. The women were mostly from Jabbar's family, and some of them were Nana's and Latif's friends. Together they changed their clothing, and those who had permission, put makeup on. I saw Nana with a little bit of lipstick on her lips. She still had her scarf on, unlike Zamarod and other women, who wanted to show their hair on such a special occasion.

I was on the dance floor when Zamarod announced, "The bride is here!" She took a tambourine and led the way outside where the car was parked. The women put their hijabs back on, and as we made our way, Nana and Zamarod began to sing the song usually heard at weddings—"*Ma keh shall awardim . . .*" I could see Latif and Jabbar in the back of the car. I couldn't wait to see her face!

The moment they stepped out of the car, chocolate was thrown in the air to welcome them. Latif wore a big green scarf on her head to cover her face. Jabbar held one of her hands, and in the other she held a big bouquet of flowers. Baba walked on her side with Jabbar, who looked so nice with traditional Afghan clothing. The only men who walked in with Latif were Baba and Jabbar. When they arrived, Latif and Jabbar stood together against the couch.

Zamarod took off the green scarf, and my eyes couldn't believe how beautiful Latif was with the gorgeous crystal dress, styled hair, and makeup. Once Jabbar sat, Latif followed him. Nana stopped singing and brought out a big cake and placed it in front of them.

As Latif had seen at other weddings, she took a special knife and held it close to the cake. She waited for Jabbar to put his hand over hers to cut the cake. Everyone clapped after the first cut. The bride and groom picked up their forks and filled them with cake. Latif had to put the cake in Jabbar's mouth first, and then Jabbar did the same for Latif. I was amazed how well Latif remembered the traditions with no preparation.

Once Jabbar and Latif performed all the necessary practices, they were asked to dance. Women from every corner of the room rushed onto the dance floor to give the bride and groom money, as was expected. I begged Nana to give me some money so I could give it to Latif. She took some money from her bra and gave it to me—enough so that Latif could buy an ice cream. I made my way to the dance floor and gave it to Latif. She smiled at me and my heart filled with joy.

Once Jabbar left, women took off their hijabs to dance. Some wore short skirts with no pants on—something that we had seen in the movies and that Baba disapproved of. There was so much to look at, but only one part of the room looked astonishing, and that was Latif. Once I saw an empty spot next to her, I ran to sit there. She was happy to see me. She ran her fingers through my hair to untangle it—even on her wedding day, she felt responsible to fix my look! Once Zia joined me, the fun began. We ate cake and sat back to watch the women dancing. Only one of them did something different; the rest danced the same moves and wouldn't sit down until the song was over.

Soon Razeq announced lunchtime in a loud voice: "*Yalah*, we are bringing food now!" He gave the women enough time to put on their hijabs. There was so much to eat, including meat, rice, eggplant, and salad, but Zia and I stuck with the cake.

While everyone ate, the music was turned off to pay respect to the angels who were present. I'd never seen them, but Baba told us many times that when we begin eating, angels join us. He had no response when I asked him how he knew that the angels didn't like music. How did he even know they were there? He didn't know, he said. His parents had told him that, along with the Akhunds from different mosques.

The dance and jubilation went on for several hours until it

got darker and the guests realized it was time for them to leave. Those who had come from far away gave Latif kisses on the cheek and wished her happiness before they left. About four or five families stayed over to celebrate the last ceremony the following day.

No one was allowed to go to our house since Nana had put in so much work to make the place look nice for Latif and Jabbar to sleep together for the first time. Nana put the mattress in the hall and put a small white sheet on the mattress. We left once Nana helped Latif to take off her rented wedding dress.

We all stayed at Zamarod's house, where the women had no interest in resting, but I put my head on Nana's lap to sleep. The hustle and bustle woke me up in the morning. There was no breakfast, so I had leftovers from the day before and waited for Latif to arrive. Once again, some of the guests rushed to wear their most presentable dresses and put makeup on to welcome Latif. There was no music, but women played the tambourine and sang.

Jabbar escorted Latif to our room and left to be with the men. Latif still looked very beautiful and was wearing a green dress, which brides often wore after the wedding day. A few minutes passed, and then the home goods that Nana and Jabbar had purchased were brought to the room so they could be announced and everyone could see what Latif was given to start her new life. "A set of kitchen knives, from her family," Nana said, as she held the set up so everyone in the room could see and clap. "One set of kitchen pans, utensils, cups, containers, and . . ." Nana announced each gift. That was usually my least favorite part of a wedding—to name every gift given. But it was a tradition; people wanted to know what the bride had gotten.

"And here is her *dastmal*." Nana showed everyone the small sheet that she had put on the mattress, but now it had blood on it. Everyone clapped for Latif and congratulated her again. In the weddings I remember, they did the same thing, and if the girl came out without a bloody *dastmal*, it meant that she was not a good girl. That was Nana's explanation to me when I asked her why there was blood on the sheet: Latif was a good woman. But was Jabbar a good man?

11

Afghanistan in the Other Life

Without Latif at home, I felt like I had so much freedom but also much more responsibility. Zia had to replace Latif, and I had to be Zia. Nana cooked often but had Zia and me observe how much oil, spices, and other things were needed. "How do you know when your rice is ready?" Nana quizzed Zia, helping her to review her cooking lessons.

"I put a grain of rice on my finger, and if I can break it easily, it means it is ready to put it in low heat to soften." Zia's response made Nana happy; she'd learned quickly.

Going to school became more challenging. I could find a way to leave the house without being noticed only when Latif or others visited. But I was still named one of the top students who could read and write the alphabet and several words in a short amount of time. I even knew the whole sentence, "Father gave water." I could read and write it without taking much time. When I wrote it for Ms. Zahra, she said she was proud of me—"*Afarin beh to!*"—something that I had never heard from Nana or Baba.

One day, I made my way to the mosque, and only students were there. No one knew where Ms. Rahmati was. We assumed she was sick, but weeks went by and there was no sign of her. I cried: the only door for us had closed, and we didn't even know why.

Since I was still an illegal immigrant, there was no point in trying to find a seat in public school. The last day I went and knocked on the door of the mosque, no one opened it for me. Was she still even alive? I wondered. Where was her house? How could I learn more without her?

Once Ms. Rahmati was gone, schooling was replaced with cooking. Nana thought a girl with no education could get suitors, but if she couldn't cook, she was of no use as a wife. Being a good cook was better than being literate, I heard, and so I slowly lost interest in learning. I too wanted to be good and to receive all the compliments Zia was getting for her cooking.

Nana and Baba reminded me that there was no need for me to know how to write names. Soon I would be married, and learning to write my husband's name was no accomplishment if I couldn't make him food.

But Nana wasn't such a bad teacher. She taught us mainly in the kitchen and complimented us when the food wasn't too oily or salty.

One day, once Zia was done cooking and I was done with my chores, we decided to lock the door and watch Naser's rented VCR tapes. He never let us watch the parts where the girl and boy danced together. But on our own, we could speed up the film and stop it when the dancing happened. It was our day: Nana went to see a doctor, and Zia and I had control of the film.

"I want to be her," said Zia, pointing at the female character with the most beautiful dress. "I want to be her too," I said. Zia had a problem with both of us wanting to be the same girl, so we flipped through the film, but I couldn't find anyone else I wanted to be. So we decided that she would be the girl, and I would be the guy, even though I was much shorter than her.

We played the song we liked the most and imitated everything in a poor way, including kissing. It was so much fun to dance with Zia and think that she was my girlfriend. She did a good job portraying that she loved me, but I didn't play the male character very well.

Then I heard a knock on the door, and we rushed to put away everything. It was Latif and Jabbar. Latif's belly was bigger; the last time I had seen her, no one could tell she was pregnant. Jabbar had gained weight. Zia and I had changed too—we had grown up so fast and could make tea and cook food with some guidance from Nana. Soon everyone else arrived and smiled when they saw Latif and Jabbar.

"What a great night you picked to visit us," Razeq said. "I rented this film days ago and was able to keep it until tonight!" I couldn't recognize the letters on the cover because they were all written in a different language, not Farsi or Hindi, which I had seen in many movies.

Razeq turned on the TV and played the film. It was totally different from what we had seen before. There were tall blond girls in the film that looked like Ranjita's doll. The language was nothing I had ever heard before. But I still continued to watch, hoping to understand the story through the characters' body language. I asked Razeq to update me on the story.

"I think a spider bit that guy, so now he has become a *mard ankaboti* [Spider-Man]," said Naser. Like Zaher, I wished for a spider to bite me so I could fly like the main character.

Soon Latif left the kitchen to join us since we couldn't stop talking about how much beauty was in the film. The tall buildings were like nothing we had seen in our lives. Where was the place with those buildings and tall blond women who looked like dolls?

"Which country is this?" Latif asked.

"Probably Afghanistan in the other life," said Razeq and laughed with the others.

In that film I saw main characters kiss for real, unlike in Bollywood movies. Although Baba disapproved of their act, he still followed the story until the end, after which everyone complimented Razeq on his film selection, and as darkness fell, the house became unbearably cold, letting us know that another winter was coming. Once we managed to turn on the heater, we gathered around the tablecloth for dinner. Even at dinner, we talked about the film.

"Maybe you should name your child Mard Ankaboti, ha-ha," said Khaleq when Latif asked us to brainstorm girl and boy names.

"Sadly, you might not be able to see the baby," Latif told us, "as Jabbar and I will be leaving Mashhad to go to Tehran, where Jabbar's job has been transferred."

Baba and Nana listed a few reasons why Latif should stay until she delivered the baby, but Jabbar assured Nana that his family in Tehran would take good care of her. Latif looked happy and trusted Jabbar with her life. Even on her last night with us, she insisted on cooking and cleaning. She wanted to take care of us until we saw her again.

When Latif left in the morning, the first snow arrived. I felt sad watching it, sad to see Latif leaving again. Nana once said that when she got married, she barely got to see her mother or father, so she had to learn to live far away from them. I wondered when I would see Latif again.

That winter, Zia and I often prayed quietly for Baba to go to the mosque sooner and come back later so we could watch something on TV other than Baba's favorite channel, which focused on God and the Quran. When Baba would leave, Zia and I recited a few verses from the Quran that we had memorized, asking God to forgive us for having more interest in watching cartoons. Sometimes I read the verses twice to make the prayer more effective.

One afternoon I walked with Baba to a new mosque, where he had recently begun to pray. Baba put his Afghan dress on and a jacket over it. "Baba, are you going outside with your Afghan clothing?" I asked.

Baba nudged his head and led the way. I was worried. "What if they find out we are Afghans?" I asked, holding his cold hand to guide him.

"I hope they already know," said Baba.

"But then they will ask us to leave their country."

"If they do, will you leave?"

"No, I like it here; I like our home," I said.

Then Baba asked me in an upset voice, "Where are you from?" He still looked unhappy when I gave him the right answer. "Home is where you don't have to hide your identity," he told me. "Home is Afghanistan." I had missed what Baba described as "home." I was missing Aziz too, as he often mentioned.

When we arrived at the mosque, Baba put his shoes in a plastic bag and walked in to find a spot. I found one next to Baba in the back of the room where I was close to the heater. There were many men in the room, and behind a thin wall, there were women and other children. The mosque felt so wonderful and warm that I thought I might not complain too much if Baba decided to stay longer than usual. Plus, I was interested to know what happened to the prophet Ibrahim, whom the imam was discussing when we walked in. I had heard his name before but never knew his story.

"When the Holy Prophet Ibrahim was condemned to be thrown into the fire, he uttered the words *Hasbi Allah wa tawakkalto ali Allah*, saying, 'God is sufficient for me in any case, and I don't care about anything else,'" said the imam. "The story highlights the profound trust in and reliance on God that Ibrahim displayed. He had complete faith in God's protection and provision, and his trust turned the fire into a garden of flowers." Old and young in the mosque listened carefully, like I did. Some were crying to hear the hardship Ibrahim had to endure, but I felt so entertained—the same way I had felt when Aziz's mother-in-law, Bibi, told me stories. Baba rolled his *tasbih* and listened to the imam.

Then the imam ended the story because it was time to pray. Each person made their way to a recessed wall shelf and grabbed a rounded clay stone to put on their prayer rugs. I took one and put it on my prayer rug. I thought it was fun to bend and touch the rock with my forehead.

"This is only for Shias. Put it back!" said Baba as he took the rock away from me. After that, I found no joy in praying.

On the way home I told Baba I wanted to be like Ibrahim—to not feel pain or be scared of fire. "We all do," he said, "but you have to be so close to Allah to help you feel no pain."

"Are you close to Allah?"

"I do whatever it takes to be close to him—as close as he is with you, with every other kid," Baba said.

I asked, “He is closer to me?”

“Yes, remember, you are innocent and just started your quest to seek him, so don’t miss the opportunity. Pray every day, don’t lie, don’t be unkind to others, and don’t forget to speak to Allah by praying every day, and if you would like him to speak to you, listen to the Quran.”

When we reached home, Nana was in the common room listening to the Quran, and I joined her. Then I asked Baba, “Why doesn’t Allah speak Farsi, Baba?” He smiled and said, “Why don’t you learn his language?” Nana and Baba believed that everything we heard in God’s language, Arabic, was a great opportunity for us to wash our sins away. I wasn’t sure how much sin we all had, so I decided to listen and hope that just by listening to all the strange words, my sins would wash away.

The next few days, I rushed Baba to take bigger steps; I didn’t want to miss the stories the imam told. Before long, I loved going to the mosque with or without Baba, who soon became too ill to leave home. Zia often encouraged me to visit the mosque since after every prayer, I took her as many sweets as I could fit in my pockets.

“Don’t put the clay rock on your prayer rug,” Baba often reminded me before I left, even though I’d become quite good at the practice.

Although Nana thought I was a godly girl, it was the power of the new stories that pulled me to the mosque in rain and snow. In fact, I was interested in becoming Ibrahim and eventually Allah, who was so mighty—more powerful than I had remembered him in Afghanistan. But wanting to be God was a great sin, Baba said, so I slowly gave up on that idea and wanted to be his friend instead.

The hero of each story became a hero just by obeying God. Was that all I needed to do to become a hero? I could do that.

I started wearing a scarf whenever I could remember and tried to not be so angry at some of the kids who bullied me and Zia. As I enjoyed free sweets at the mosque, I listened to the stories. Some people around me still cried, while in my head, I gave some of the stories different endings, as I had with Bibi's stories.

Although I thought going to the mosque and praying in my own way was sufficient, Baba insisted that I must learn the Quran in order to be a true friend to Allah. So he became my teacher—way better than the Akhund. Although I never understood a word of what I learned, I felt accomplished whenever I recognized verses being recited during the mosque prayers. I could have memorized more verses if Baba's sickness had not completely taken away his strength to teach.

As Baba got sicker, Nana couldn't take him to the hospital because they often asked undocumented refugees for extra papers and money and we couldn't always ask Ms. Zahra to do a favor for us. So our house became a hospital, with one patient and several nurses, who couldn't ease his pain. I was in charge of taking the plastic wash basin to Baba; Nana and Zia were in charge of making soft food; and my brothers were in charge of making enough money for the medication and giving Baba a bath when necessary. He needed a lot of attention and often cried.

Baba cried for something sweet—for home, for Afghanistan. No matter how hard Nana tried to make Baba feel better, he still feared dying in Iran, where people and the government denied us even when we were alive.

As months passed, Nana, who had tried all kinds of medicine, came to the conclusion that the main remedy to cure Baba was the air of Herat. When Baba heard Nana accepting what he needed the most, he did not say much. He did cry less, or maybe his tears had dried out.

"He should be resting, not traveling back to Afghanistan," said Ms. Zahra, hoping to change Nana's mind. But it was too late; we had sold most of our belongings to go home. I could have sworn that we had a home in Iran—the house we had found in Mashhad, the house where we heard no gunshots and that never failed to keep us safe during harsh seasons. But Nana said that Baba had left his heart in Herat. We had to return to find it for him so he could feel alive again.

When we were packed up and ready to leave, Ms. Zahra said, "You must visit me when you return." She hugged us for the last time and waved until the car drove us away.

Who was going to carry Baba through the tall mountains and cold? It would have to be Razeq or Zaher, since Naser and Khaleq decided to stay in Iran to work. I feared returning to the roads we once had struggled to pass. But to my surprise, we didn't need to take that same route.

Instead, we reported ourselves as undocumented refugees and asked to be deported. Baba's illness helped us cut the line and get on the bus as soon as it arrived. We put our few belongings in the luggage compartment where we once had hidden to travel to Iran. In just a short time, the bus was filled with Afghans. The bus driver told us that it should take only about six hours to get to Herat if there weren't any problems. I think that if someone had told Baba that Herat was only six hours away from us, he would have visited Aziz sooner. Those two or three years, Afghanistan had felt like it was on the other side of the world.

The bus stopped and gave everyone a chance to pray, use the bathroom, or eat. People who could afford it made their way to restaurants nearby, but we had to rely on whatever Nana had packed for us. As we ate, Nana learned other people's stories. Most of them claimed to be missing Afghanistan. Some had to return to Afghanistan because their family's breadwinner had been deported.

When we were back on the road, I kept looking outside the window, wondering when the tall buildings and paved roads would end. I was impatient to see the Karbar, Aziz, and Ranjita.

Nana and Razeq talked about staying at Aziz's house for a few days until we found a place to live. It had been such a long time: all these years, Aziz had no news from us. No one had cell phones at that time; there was no way to stay in touch. She would be so happy to see us all alive.

After a short nap, Zia and I began to make up stories, stopping only when we saw a sign for Afghanistan. Someone saw a flag—green, red, black. It was an Afghan flag, which I had never seen before. Then I saw more proof that we were in Afghanistan: several women with burqas, and children with dusty clothes running around to sell snacks and other goods. Baba was finally wide awake, asking Nana to share whatever she saw. But there wasn't much to see besides the tall dusty mountains and sometimes small villages.

Once the bus got closer to Herat, I saw the people I'd seen on TV—the armed American soldiers walking on the streets and sitting on the backs of cars. *Are they going to kill us?* I wondered. Their faces weren't too different from the people we saw on the news and in the film *Spider-Man*.

"You have arrived," said the driver and opened the door for us. My heart began to beat faster. I was scared to see more soldiers a few steps away from us. I wasn't sure if they were making eye contact since they were all wearing sunglasses, but they didn't hurt us. I guess they were different from the Taliban fighters.

They watched us as we took our belongings from the compartment and waited to find a taxi. I saw a *shiryakh* seller and ran toward his cart. In Iran I ate many ice creams, but none tasted like *shiryakh.* How could I choose Iran over Afghanistan, where I grew up with the sweetest taste I could remember? We rushed to eat our treat and then sat in a taxi to go to Aziz's house.

On the way, I recognized several markets, stores, and alleys. I also saw a group of girls in white and black uniforms. Was it true that girls could go to school now? If that was correct, I'd join them as soon as I could! I felt so excited that I stuck my head outside the car's window. There was so much to see.

"The American soldiers are the reason why you don't see public executions in the city anymore," said the driver.

Razeq continued asking more questions about the soldiers, Herat, work opportunities, kite running, and music. "Do the American soldiers let you play music?" he asked after hearing several rickshaws and cars passing by and playing music out loud. We were so happy to hear that dancing and music were no longer prohibited. Since Baba couldn't see such changes with his own failing eyes, Razeq reported every important change he saw. Some parts of Herat now looked as clean as Mashhad. As we entered the heart of the city, I saw more women and girls shopping. I even saw some girls Zia's age without scarves.

When we arrived, Nasim, Aziz's daughter, saw us, quit playing, and ran to the house. Nana smiled and let Baba know. Aziz swiftly made her way to see for herself that we were back, alive.

She cried just like when we had left. Her sister-in-law watched us from the first floor and smiled. Ata made his way to the yard where we all stood. Aziz gave each of us a long hug and kiss as she cried.

Baba cried Aziz's name and hugged her. "Aziz, Aziz!" Aziz looked so heartbroken when she saw Baba looking for the kids with his hands since his eyes could not help him.

Ata welcomed us and helped Razeq put our belongings in their basement.

Although Aziz looked different, thinner, she was still the same, kind and welcoming. She smiled, as she poured cups of tea for us, when she heard about Latif being happily married.

"Baba, did you like Iran?" asked Aziz. Baba thought a little, and his eyes began to fill with tears. Aziz received her answer.

"He missed you, Sister, we all did!" said Razeq.

"I am thankful that God granted me the greatest wish I had—seeing you once again," said Aziz.

Once tea was served, Nana brought the big suitcase that had souvenirs for Aziz, Ata, and their kids. "This bowl is from Imam Reza, a healer, the descendant of the prophet Muhammad," Nana said.

None of us could understand what was written in the golden bowl, which shone like Imam Reza's shrine, but Nana assumed it was phrases from the Quran. Aziz loved it. More than the bowl, she also loved the crystal-studded sandals that Nana brought for her and Nasim. For Ata, Nana had a box of *gaz* (nougat) with pistachio on it. He opened it and took two; his kids and I ate all the rest.

While the adults were busy talking, Zia, Nasim, and I left the house to visit the Karbar. Nasim led the way as she spoke of her greatest achievement: catching the biggest fish she had ever seen. "Can you swim yet?" asked Zia. It would have been so cool if that was also one of her achievements, since none of us could swim.

"I can read," I said, but Zia wasn't very impressed with my achievement because I could read only certain words, not everything. To prove Zia wrong, I looked for a sign to read. Unlike Iran, there were no signs anywhere on the streets or on walls to read.

I quit arguing with Zia when I saw the Karbar. I ran to it and found the shallow part, where Ranjita and I used to fish. It felt shallower, as if it had shrunk, or maybe I had grown up. It still appeared to be a joyful playground for kids as I heard clapping and singing and saw children chasing each other, just like before. While Herat had changed, the Karbar was still the same, fun and playful. The little rocks in the riverbed felt like a soft carpet. I felt as if finally, I was home.

The mosque's white walls had faded, but they still stood strong and tall. While Nasim and Zia were playing, I ran up the hill that led to our old alley. I hoped to see Ranjita seated on her carpet, but I saw no one. The door looked rusted, as if no one was living there anymore. I was tempted to knock on the door but didn't. I looked at our old house and left soon after.

We rented a house near the Karbar and a school, but Nana disliked the idea of education even more when Aziz reported that many girls were being kidnapped on the way to and from school. Despite their worries, I still found a place called "home school." It wasn't as far as the real one, but I could go late and come back when I felt I should. The teacher was Latif's age.

She gave us free notebooks, colored pencils, books, and even a backpack. There were about ten kids, and the rest of the room was filled with elders.

Many women were in burqas in class to hide their identities so they wouldn't be reported to their families. Ata's brother thought that women and girls who became educated acted like wild dogs, impossible to put back on a leash. The reason why they wanted to learn reading and writing, he said, was to send their lovers letters.

I thought he was wrong because I had no lover and I still wanted to learn. I wanted to make Baba and Nana proud, but how could I when they both disapproved?

As my teacher recommended, I never shared anything about school with my family until the day I got a perfect grade on my writing exam—the only one in the class who got a perfect grade. The whole class clapped for me when the teacher said my name and rewarded me with a beautiful pack of colored pencils.

I ran home, so excited for Zia to hear that I spilled the secret in front of Nana. "So you lied that you went to play with Aziz's kids?" she said with anger. "No more going out!" To avoid making her more upset, I made my way to the common room.

I found Baba in the corner of the room, near a big window. He was still motionless on his mattress, looking paler than the day before. I put my lips close to Baba's ears and whispered, "I got a perfect score on my writing exam!" I didn't expect Baba to say anything. I felt bad for him for being stuck in the corner of the room, where the flies didn't give him any peace. I began to like Baba even more because, after Zia, he was the only one who listened to me; he had become my patient stone.

Once the sun began to set, I was assigned to clean the yard

and then put the dusty handmade rug in the middle of the yard, just like before. We were missing Latif, Naser, and Khaleq, but it felt like the old days when we used to gather together and drink black tea with cardamom. Once Razeq returned from work, he carried Baba to the front yard where we could keep an eye on him and chase away the flies that followed him everywhere.

12

Razeq's Engagement—and Mine

"I have found you a nice girl, she is very beautiful, white, with long hair," said Nana to Razeq. Like Zia, Zaher, and I, he giggled.

"What is her name?" Razeq asked.

"Benafsh. I saw her when we went to Shadijan village," Nana said. "She is from a good family."

"How much is *pishkash*?"

"I'm not sure," Nana said, "but I will find out more tomorrow."

"What does she look like?"

"She is as tall as Latif, but a little bigger, and I heard she is a great cook. Plus, she does embroidery on clothing," Nana said. "She cannot read or write, which should assure you that she is the right girl to have as a wife."

Nana answered all of Razeq's questions. He listened with desire and excitement and felt impatient for the morning to arrive.

In the morning, Razeq and Zaher stayed home to take care of Baba while Zia, Nana, and I made our way to Shadijan. Since Baba was sick, Nana had no choice but to meet with the father herself. On our way, Nana found a pastry shop, bargained, and purchased the most good-looking sweets and flowers.

The little guy who answered the door swiftly left and returned with a lady close to Aziz's age, but her skin was lighter. She saw the sweets and flowers and understood Nana's purpose. "Come in, please," the lady said, welcoming us. They had a big house, with a first floor meant only to keep cows, sheep, and chickens. We walked up the clay stairs, and in the upstairs room, the light of the sun appeared. The lady left the room and returned with her daughter, Benafsh.

She was so beautiful—maybe more beautiful than Marjan had been. I wished Razeq could be with us to see her.

Soon the father, with two other kids my age, joined us. He was much younger than Baba and seemed very kind. He asked Nana about our family history and who we knew in the village. Once Nana and Benafsh's father were done talking about their parents, family, and relatives, Nana began the expected conversation.

"I am here on behalf of my husband and my son to ask for your daughter's hand," said Nana and put Razeq's picture in front of Benafsh's father. Benafsh was still staring at the carpet, as the father passed the picture to the mother. Benafsh tried to look without seeming as though she were interested. After all, it didn't matter if she liked the look of him or not; her father would be the one to make the decision.

"What is his job?" asked the father.

"Construction," Nana said.

More questions: "Is he healthy? Does he pray every day?"

"He does not smoke, if that is what you are concerned about, and he does pray," said Nana. "After all, he is Muslim." I thought Nana was lying because Razeq usually prayed only when forced to.

The father asked a few other questions while Benafsh was absent. Meanwhile, I ate chocolate and played with Benafsh's sister, who was my age. I was dragged back to the adults' conversation only when I heard Nana, Benafsh's father, and her mother clapping.

On our way home, Nana bought sweets and stopped by a record shop. "Give me a CD full of happy songs for my son's engagement," said Nana. When we arrived home, Nana congratulated Razeq and put the first pastry in his mouth. "Tell me about her, Nana," said Razeq, who was very impatient.

"You will meet her once we have the first portion of the money to pay Benafsh's father," said Nana.

Once meeting Benafsh became Razeq's goal, he started working more. Suddenly Razeq became a different person; he looked happier than ever before. Every time he returned from work, he turned on music and danced. We all danced; we all felt happy, especially Nana, because she no longer had to remind Razeq to go to work and save money. He worked hard, days and weeks, until half of the *pishkash* was ready to be delivered to Benafsh's father.

Before going to Shadijan, Razeq got a haircut and shaved his beard. He dressed in the blue clothing Nana had purchased for this day. Aziz burned *esfand* seeds to ward off the evil eye and to wish Razeq good luck. In the car, I admired his appearance.

When we arrived, we were all dusty from the unpaved roads, but Razeq still stood out. As we walked toward Benafsh's house, young and old passersby stared at Razeq and, as Eid wasn't near, probably knew he was going to be married.

"Welcome everybody, please come in!" Benafsh's father guided us to the guest room. He looked much cleaner and more excited than the first time we had met him. "This handsome man must be Razeq Jan," he said, giving Razeq a hug. A few minutes passed, and then Benafsh's mother and sister joined us with tea and sweets. Excited by the possibility of having a new friend, I may have felt happier than Razeq.

Once I had enough sweets, I left the room to find the younger sister. She wasn't much fun, but it was better than sitting in the other room where the adults even bored themselves with their dull conversations.

Soon the Akhund arrived to witness Razeq and Benafsh being engaged. Benafsh was called to the guest room, joined by her relatives. When she came into the room, everyone clapped and threw chocolate in her way. Razeq was so drowned in Benafsh's beauty that he forgot to clap.

Razeq, eighteen years old, and his bride, Benafsh, sixteen years old, in Afghanistan.

"Sit next to the groom," the Akhund said to Benafsh. Razeq opened up space for her, looking quickly at her face before staring at the rug like Benafsh.

"Do you accept Miss Ahmadi as your wife?" the Akhund asked Razeq, the same phrase three times. Once Razeq and Benafsh were religiously affiliated, the room filled with joy and laughter. We stayed the night at Benafsh's family home, where Razeq's celebration took place. During the whole celebration, Razeq and Benafsh exchanged only one word: "Salaam." They were too shy, but by the morning, the strangers had become best friends. They were given permission to stay alone for a short time. I could hear Razeq laughing the way he used to with Marjan. He sang and danced for all those years he had been silenced.

Zia and I got beautiful dresses (which we sold shortly after Razeq and Benafsh's small wedding to have extra money for rent and Baba's medication). As the weeks had gone by, Baba appeared less alive, even though he took his medications. One afternoon, I was telling Baba of my new lesson and how special I felt because I could finally read.

"On this paper it's written: 'Zaki helps his father to put apples in the box.' " I wasn't expecting Baba to say anything—it was actually okay to have a father who only listened; the rest of the family liked speaking more than listening. It was a hot afternoon, and he began to breathe abnormally. I was still reading when Baba's hand twitched and he began to inhale heavily.

Although I was sweating because of the heat, Baba felt cold to me. He opened his eyes and, with difficulty, called our names. Nana quit cooking and rushed to the bag of medication. She picked some pills that she thought to be the right ones and tried to give them to Baba, but she gave up because he had no energy to swallow a pill. "Hurry, go find the Akhund," Nana said to me, and she told Razeq to run to Aziz's house.

When I returned with the Akhund, Aziz was there, crying and kissing Baba's hand. "Is Baba dying?" I asked Zia, who wasn't sure what was happening. Razeq stood by the door and wiped away tears. Baba called the names of Naser, Khaleq, and Latif several times. He had forgotten that they were in Iran.

"Sonita . . ." I left the corner of the room when I heard Baba calling for me. I felt scared, scared of Baba. "Hold his hand," said Nana. I held Baba's hand and looked at him as he was slowly leaving us. I wished I could cry, so Baba would feel that I was sad for his departure. Why couldn't I cry? *I like you a lot, Baba*, I said in my head as my lips and brain were shut down.

"Baba, *mano halal kon*." Razeq, Nana, and Aziz asked Baba for forgiveness while the Akhund cited the verses of the Quran that I had heard before at a funeral. "*Behest jaygay to bashad*." The Akhund repeated the same phrase over and over to assure Baba he was going to heaven. As Baba slowly ran out of breath, the cries increased.

Baba slowly stopped calling names. He had to leave to return his soul to God. I watched Baba taking his last breath. "Baba?" Aziz called. He wasn't there anymore in the motionless body. My first and last tear sat on my cheek. It was over, Baba was gone.

I began to really believe the phrase, "Life can be ended in the blink of an eye." Where could I find Baba if I missed him? I don't know how many more questions came to my mind until I forced myself to accept the reality. I wished I could have given Baba my share of life so that he could stay alive longer; we had been becoming good friends.

Then I returned to the present, where Baba's body appeared

relaxed. He left without even taking his *tasbih*, the most important part of his daily prayer. Nana gave it to the Akhund with some wrinkled cash.

When Baba left, the doors were kept open for different forms of sadness.

Soon, hunger became our neighbor once again. Gradually, our tablecloth grew lighter, and one by one, our household belongings vanished. Fortunately, we hadn't sold all our fine dresses; Zia and I wore them to hide how poor we were.

Slowly becoming poor felt like a discovery: we explored every possible way to survive. A favorite thing that Zia and I did was to attend other people's weddings and act as if we knew the bride or the groom. It was stressful, but we were successful.

"Show me your invitation," asked the guard standing in front of the door.

"Our mother is waiting for us in the salon," Zia lied.

"There are no women in the venue yet," the guard said, holding his gun and examining our elegant outfits, which took the focus off our dusty, broken slippers. But then he asked us, "Do you come here to dance or to eat?"

"To eat," Zia told him, telling him the truth, which warmed his heart.

"Nothing in this world is for free. If I let you go eat, what would you give the groom?" He laughed and playfully directed his question at Zia.

"Umm, we don't have money," said Zia.

"Money is not the only way that you girls can pay. What else can you offer?" he asked again.

Our most valuable items were our clothing and a plastic ring that I had found in a snack bag. "Do you want this?" I took my ring and held it in front of him. He was not impressed. Without giving us another chance to evaluate all our assets, he said, "Pay with dancing and bringing more joy to the event. No screaming or chasing other kids around—dance and clap. Go ahcad."

Zia and I were the first people to arrive at the event. Only a few cleaning ladies were there, preparing the tables. Zia ran on the stage, where a beautiful large red couch was located for the bride and groom. The stage was decorated with flowers and lights. Zia sat on the couch; I followed her.

"I'm the bride," said Zia, laughing. We used the moment to rehearse our own wedding day. "You're the groom; put my veil up!"

I put up Zia's imaginary veil. Before our wedding was official, the cleaning lady interrupted us. "Leave the stage, you two," she said in an angry voice.

Soon guests filled the venue. Zia and I did exactly what the guard had told us not to do. We ran and chased other kids, and sometimes danced too.

Our favorite part was lunch, when they brought me and Zia large plates of rice and meat. We ate less than what our stomachs begged for and put the leftovers in a black plastic bag to take home. Zia and I thought that the wedding venue felt like the way heaven was described: colorful, full of beautiful faces, and filled with plates of food.

That venue became our favorite place, and the guard became our friend. Like us, several other girls attended weddings uninvited. Sometimes it was embarrassing to see them there. We all wore the same overused dresses each time, while other girls our age wore gorgeous dresses and women had gold hanging from their necks. At every wedding we saw different looks and dresses. But the bride's sad face was always the same—even though marriage was the ultimate goal for every boy and girl.

One day, before lunchtime, Zia and I put on our dresses and meticulously brushed our hair. We looked quite fancy and ready to blend in with the rest of the elegant wedding guests. We left the house with excitement and walked the road that led to the wedding venue. But rushing upstairs, we noticed an unusual lack of music bouncing from the venue.

The moment Zia and I stepped inside the hall, we were met with the hushed sobs of women. How embarrassing!—we had dressed for a wedding and accidently walked into a funeral. Zia grabbed my hand as we quickly made our way toward the stairs.

Once we were home, Zia shared with Nana what had happened. "Ha-ha! This will always be my favorite story," she said, laughing out loud with Benafsh. We returned empty-handed, but our mishap fed Nana's soul with laughter—something that we needed more than food.

After that we no longer visited the wedding venue. Zia was getting closer to the age of twelve, which was considered a suitable time for a girl to start building a better reputation. Afghanistan appeared safer than before, but our family showed no interest in embracing change. Although at about age ten I had no restrictions, in just a short time, my freedom began to shrink and my value began to rise.

One afternoon, I returned home to find Aziz and her daughter. Before I could embrace Nasim, Aziz quietly directed me to the kitchen. "Go wash your face," she said as she brushed my hair with her fingers and put a scarf on my head.

As I splashed cold fresh well water on my face, I saw Zia and Zaher standing under the little window and listening to the adult conversation exchanged in the room. Curious, I abandoned my efforts and rushed to join them. "He is a hardworking young man," I managed to hear.

"Who's in the room?" I asked quietly. Zaher shushed me with a big smile on his face.

"Sonita is the right age . . ." I pressed my ears against the wall, listening carefully until I heard them discussing departure. As the guests prepared to leave the room, Zia and Zaher ran to the kitchen, and I followed them.

The three of us giggled, hiding behind the tattered kitchen curtain, which was black with smoke. We poked additional holes into the curtain at our eye level and saw three ladies in burqas. Just as I began to focus on the heavy lady's shiny dress visible beneath her long hijab, Zia abruptly took my position so I lost sight of our unexpected guests.

Then I heard the door bang and Nana came into the kitchen. "You might be a bride soon," she said to me with a smile on her face, "so you better learn to act like one." Zia and Zaher jumped up and down, but I was confused.

"I'm a bride?! When is my wedding?" I asked. Aziz and Nana laughed as they looked at me.

Even though I was confused, I was excited too. I was going to receive new clothing and even gold earrings and maybe rings! Nana responded with advice: "A proper girl would not show too much excitement to be married off because people might think you have always been looking for a husband."

Then Nana and I walked into the hall, where I saw a box of sweets and flowers, much fresher than what Latif had received. I rushed to the box of sweets. Before I could put a second sweet in my mouth, Nana complained about my behavior. She wanted a ten-year-old girl to act like a thirty-year-old woman.

"If they see you behaving like a five-year-old, they might choose anyone but you. That means you could lose all the excitement of being a bride in a nice venue and having nice clothing," said Nana. I decided that I would force myself to become a different person—someone who didn't eat too much and was able to do more housework.

Nana took a sip of tea. "You are lucky that your husband is only Zaher's age," Aziz said. "By the time he is ready to start a family, you will be a lady, ready to make us proud." Aziz's words planted the idea in my head, which was filled with beautiful dresses.

After that, all I could think about was going outside to tell my friends that I was actually a bride now—just like how we played in our games. I had no freedom to change my role, but it didn't bother me, as I had learned from other girls that being a bride was a big achievement.

Nana shook my shoulder to bring me back to her lecture. "Do you understand what I'm saying?" she asked. "Yes!" I responded with a big smile, listening carefully to Nana and all her requirements, one of which was cutting out my playtime and staying inside the house.

A few days passed, and every day I managed to age one year, bringing joy to Nana. Sometimes, even Zia lectured me on the lessons of growing up faster. Zia had learned the lessons very well and could have been the bride instead of me. But she was too close to the groom's age; the bride always had to be two to four years younger than the groom.

Although Zia had to wait longer for the exciting moment of her life to be chosen, she felt like a bride too when we all went shopping to prepare for my engagement. Nana borrowed money from Aziz's husband and first bought rice and flour. Then she purchased beautiful red, shiny shoes, which never had been even in my dreams, and a long green scarf, which every bride had to wear on her engagement day.

I wore my red shoes, put on the green scarf, and walked around the room. Razeq entered the hall with a bucket of grapes brought from his in-laws' farm. He laughed and popped grapes into his mouth. I joined him and chuckled at my silliness.

"Let me help you," said Razeq, as he held my hand and walked me around the common room. It was such a short rehearsal with Razeq, but I'd never forget the amount of joy it brought me in that moment.

Unlike Nana, Razeq was okay with my laughing and being excited about my wedding. I loved it when he teased me, saying, "My Sister—who could guess that one day you too will be a bride?" and then he would laugh.

But this time of such joy was followed by a terrifying event.

Only a few days after the engagement preparations, Razeq was injured in a suicide bombing in the market where he had recently found a job. We all forgot about the most exciting moment of my life and spent days at the hospital, where we spent all the money we had and borrowed more from people.

Nana said Razeq was reborn when, among many, he survived. The attack and fear of suicide bombings discouraged girls from going to school and breadwinners from going to their places of work.

Over time, there was less demand for Razeq's job, which involved construction. The most popular occupation became undertaker, since suicide bombings were killing more and more people.

13

Return to Iran

Just after I had proudly told the girls in our neighborhood about my upcoming wedding, it was called off. My heart broke at the thought of not being a bride in a beautiful wedding dress. I blamed my family, and they blamed the instability that forced many Afghans to either flee—or perish.

Once again we sold all our belongings. Benafsh wasn't happy to see all her household gifts from her family and Nana be sold just to help us all find a way back to Iran. And Zaher said, "I'm not going anywhere." But we all went anyway: Nana, me, Zia, Zaher, and Razeq and Benafsh.

But I was thrilled by the idea of going back to Iran, although I didn't like the idea of the long journey. After several days, Nana told us that we wouldn't go the long way this time. By paying extra to the officers who would do anything for more money, we all had passports and visas granted to us. We were going back to Iran by bus, the same way we'd returned to Afghanistan.

I looked at the thin blue passport with our pictures in it. How sad—we'd sold our entire lives to get this weightless book, and Nana still feared that it might not buy us entry into Iran.

This time, Aziz didn't cry as much, maybe because she knew we would make it back again, like we had before. Nana gave Aziz her last tears—all she had left to give her beloved daughter.

"*Yallah, yallah!*" The bus driver's call demanded the attention of all the passengers. Everyone rushed to hug little ones, said their goodbyes, and stopped bargaining with the children my age selling biscuits, bread, and water.

I climbed aboard, and through the dusty window of the bus, I waved at Nasim and Aziz until I could no longer see them. I leaned my head against the window, ate the small piece of bread Nana had given me for lunch, and listened to the conversations around me.

"Tell me more about Iran, is it nice?"

"Yeah, but the people are fucking racists."

When we reached the Iranian police checkpoint, the police officer looked at our passports, starting from the back of the bus, and asked everyone the same question: "What is the reason for your trip to Iran?"

The police officer asked this without looking in the eyes of one old man. "My wife needs heart surgery," he said. "We are going to Iran for medical treatment." Almost 90 percent of the people on the bus made medical treatment their reason for visiting. It wasn't too hard; the police officer looked at papers that had been written by paid doctors.

"What is your reason for your trip to Iran?" the officer asked Nana.

"We are going to visit Imam Reza's shrine," she said.

"How long will you be there?"

"Just thirty days."

"Who are these kids?"

"My children."

"What is your name?" the officer asked me.

"Sonita." The police officer looked at the passport page where my name and picture were and returned the passport to Nana. Once he moved to the seats in front of us, we began to breathe again.

As soon as the bus passed the final police checkpoint, several passengers threw their medical papers into the air and celebrated their entry into Iran. The once somber bus transformed into a party on wheels. We all celebrated—mainly me. I knew that we were back in Iran the moment dusty roads turned into asphalt and I saw girls in pink school uniforms. We'd arrived! I heard the passengers who were seeing Iran for the first time saying nothing but "Wow" as they looked out the bus windows.

Once the bus stopped in a big terminal, everyone took their belongings. Some seemed to know where they were going, and some appeared to be lost—no home, no friends, in a big new country. We were lucky to be among the few who had a place to go—where Latif lived, in Tehran. When we arrived there, I saw women in short hijabs, with red lipstick and even long painted nails. Flowers were everywhere. People looked so clean—much more so than in Mashhad.

We had to take a taxi to Latif's house, and we found one whose driver didn't mind that there were more of us than seats. I sat on Nana's lap and looked out the window. As time passed, the taxi took us away from the beautiful bustling city to a town that appeared somewhat impoverished and dusty. The moment it stopped, Latif ran to us, and, behind her, a little girl followed.

Latif cried out loud not to see Baba with us, because she hadn't known that he had died. Once she had enough of crying,

Left to right: My oldest brother, Naser, me, and Nana after arriving in Tehran.

she greeted us and told her little daughter, Fadia, to give us a hug. I immediately fell in love with her, and I held her hand as Latif led the way into her house. The place smelled like Latif's cooking, with so many spices and garlic.

Latif's house wasn't impressive, nowhere close to where we had lived in Mashhad, but she looked happy. Latif had changed. She was skinnier but still kind and clearly loved us so much. While everyone was helping her prepare food, Nana and I played joyfully with Fadia, only stopping when Jabbar walked in. He looked much older and less attractive than when he had left us in Mashhad. He greeted us and hurried to the bathroom to wash his hands, which were covered with black spots. Once he came back, he gave Razeq a hug and congratulated him and Benafsh on their marriage.

Thousands of old and new stories, questions, and answers were shared around the tablecloth, but Jabbar didn't respond to Razeq when he asked about his job. This question stayed unanswered until Jabbar left and Latif began to cry again—but this time not about Baba.

"The old man was right; Jabbar is a drug dealer," said Latif and dried her tears while helping Fadia brush her hair. Nana and Razeq said nothing; perhaps they felt awful for not listening to the person who had first warned us about Jabbar being a bad person.

I still wasn't sure what a drug dealer was until I saw Jabbar in action. While Latif and Nana went to get Fadia a vaccination, Jabbar stayed at home in the guest room—a place we were forbidden to enter. Jabbar called Razeq and asked me and Zia to leave the room. But I was curious, so I peeked from behind the curtain and saw several boxes of dates in the middle of the room.

Jabbar passed the dates to Razeq. At first, I thought they were going to eat them, but Jabbar told Razeq to remove all the pits. He did so and added the pitted dates to a bucket with more dates in it, mixing them together. Then Jabbar lit the gas stove and placed a small skewer in the flame. Once they were soft and resembled the sap we had cultivated in Afghanistan, Jabbar grabbed a plastic bag and filled it with dates. Then he covered the dates with a thin layer of heroin and taped around it. Jabbar took about five packages to be sold for the price of pure opium.

Benafsh told Nana that Razeq wanted to help Jabbar with his unknown activities. Nana was upset with Razeq, but she didn't show it. We couldn't be mad at Jabbar, who gave us permission to stay at his house until we found somewhere to live.

As days passed, Jabbar revealed his true self. He often screamed at Latif and smoked heroin in the same room with all of us present. The fear of Razeq becoming addicted to heroin too encouraged us to search for a new home. We found a farm, and although it was far away from Latif, other people, and schools, it was our best option. Instead of paying rent, we offered our services to keep the farm clean and fresh. The farm wasn't very big, as mostly it was the summer home for a rich family. In the winter, the mansion in the far corner of the farm would be empty, but we weren't allowed to live there. Instead, we had to live in two rooms, with a detached kitchen and a bathroom.

One part of the farm was absolutely beautiful: a swing tightly and carefully knotted to a big burry tree. The tree was surrounded by honeysuckle and roses, weakened by the heat of the sun and lack of attention. When we arrived, we revitalized the roses, giving them a new look and smell. Most of the birds in the valley visited our flowers before starting their day. Like the birds, I felt alive visiting that corner of the farm.

In the mornings, I sat on the swing with my eyes closed. I pushed it back and forth with my feet loosely touching the ground. The morning wind was fresh, the wind playfully throwing my hair back and forth each time the swing moved. The singing of the birds was a peaceful melody that I'll always remember.

A month passed before Khaleq's and Naser's full-time construction jobs allowed them to pay us a visit. Once again we were together, but without Baba and Aziz. We enjoyed the same black and green tea with cardamom and fresh, sweet homemade bread.

"I missed this, Nana," said Khaleq.

After answering a million questions that Naser and Khaleq had about Baba's passing, we all got to speak of our new life and plans to stay together. Naser and Khaleq had returned to their old jobs, looking in trash cans for plastic, paper, bread, and glass bottles. If they were lucky, they might find aluminum. They would sleep in the mornings and leave for work before the trash cans would be emptied at night, coming back around 3 or 4 a.m. with massive bags of saleable items on their backs. My favorite part was unpacking the trash bags that had gold in them—books!

They slept until midday while I dug through the bags. Some of the books were so heavy and impossible to read, but I still stole them to add to my collection—fifty-eight books in just a few days. I was able to read only three of them—the ones that didn't have difficult language. The day before the weekend, Khaleq came back with a van they had rented to bring back dozens more trash bags. People threw away more trash on the weekends, including some things they didn't mean to, like small amounts of money or jewelry.

One day, Zia found four or five new nail polishes. That day I was happy too: I found the corpse of a book—it had no cover and damaged pages, but it had some black and white images in it. Curious to know what was written in it, I sat down on the pile of trash cartons and read.

"Sonita, do your job now!" Nana interrupted my reading at exactly the moment I was dragged into the story. I wanted to know who the main character was and why her sister wanted to kill her. It was a really catchy story, so I took the book and, against Nana's will, left for my favorite part of the farm to read it.

I sat on the swing and began again, stopping only once I heard the sound of footsteps. "Nana wants you to come back and separate the cartons," Zia said, as she walked between the trees toward me. "What are you doing?"

"Shush, I am reading," I said.

"What is it?"

"It's the most beautiful story, even better than Bibi's stories!"

"Really?" Zia asked.

"Yes, do you want to hear it?"

"Yes! Read it for me from the beginning," Zia said. Since the story didn't have a beginning, I began from where I had left off and read out loud.

"Where are you two?!" we heard Nana yell. "Don't you ever run away from work again, you hear me?"

"We're reading the most beautiful story," I told her. "Do you want to hear it, Nana?"

"No, do your job," she responded. "I've heard enough stories."

Nana was never going to like reading—I knew that. But after I read Zia a few pages, she wanted to be able to read like me.

I felt a pang of sadness as I got to the end of the book; the story was growing more captivating just as I reached the final page and realized the end was missing. Zia and I scoured the trash for the remainder of the story. We checked and cleaned all the trash bags, but there was no sign of the missing tale. That night, we decided to quell the incessant questions in our minds about what happened. We reverted to our old method: we crafted an ending that satisfied us.

We lay in our bed in the yard, under the bright stars. We added additional lines until we drifted off to sleep, just before we had found the perfect ending.

Three years went by, and I made thousands of friends—the characters of each book I read. There were good and bad stories, but even in the bad ones, there was a good person, who reminded me of Ranjita, and an evil one, like the Taliban.

"Nana, why is there always good and bad in a story?" I asked. "Why can't it be just good?"

"Sometimes the two opposites are needed for us to better understand the value of each," Nana replied.

"But being bad has no value."

"You used to be mean to that guy, Shir Khan, do you remember?" she asked. "But probably you had a reason to be rude. So, even bad is not always bad; it can be not good for us, but it might bring good feelings to another person. You know I prefer all summer to have an hour of sun and the rest of the night, but the hot days also come and bring light to the flowers that love to bloom. There is always a good thing even in bad actions—maybe not for all, but for someone," said Nana, thinking that I was convinced, but I was more lost than before.

This was my daily routine: I would read useful and useless, complete and incomplete texts, and then I would go to the carpet in the middle of the farm where our afternoon family reunion would take place. After raising just one question, I would leave to play on the swing, and when I came back, I would still hear Nana, Razeq, Benafsh, Zia, Zaher, Khaleq, and Naser talking about the same question. Sometimes, I would raise a question several times, and no one would respond, as if they couldn't hear me—as if I didn't exist.

Everyone in my family thought I would stop craving my old dream of going to school since I had access to so many books, but the more I read, the stronger my yearning for school became. I wanted to go to school, but each time I asked, I was heartbroken because my desire was met with silence. One morning, I woke up and found all my books dumped in the pile of boxes to be sent to sell. I cried so much. I sat behind the mansion in the far corner of the farm and cursed as I let my tears flow: stupid Zia, stupid Razeq, stupid Nana . . . I felt as if once again I had lost Ranjita.

I protested by neglecting my tasks. I even used bathroom breaks to escape work. But a few days after the book incident, Nana gave me a new, exciting task. "Take this bread to Latif and return quickly," she said, handing me wrinkled cash for the bus. I was more than happy to leave home and see Fadia.

We lived about an hour away from Latif by foot and sometimes had to wait twenty to forty minutes for the bus to arrive. Once it did, I blended in with a family to avoid paying the cost. When I arrived, I bought myself a chocolate ice cream and walked fast enough to save the leftover ice cream for Fadia before it melted.

"So delicious!" said Fadia as she took a bite of the ice cream and Nana's homemade bread. We sat outside where the gentle wind made the hot weather bearable. We played and played until I saw it, a sign of a school—not pink uniforms this time, but blue ones. I left Latif and Fadia abruptly, following the girls; there were so many of them. After a few minutes of spying on them, I arrived at the public school. I had seen it before, but it hadn't occurred to me to try to get in. Maybe this time, they would ignore my identity and accept me in class. But once I got close to the entrance, I saw the sign: "Afghanis Aren't Allowed." So I walked away.

I wanted to find a school, so I walked to one that didn't have a sign on it. But there, they said the same thing I had heard years before: "Go away, we don't accept Afghanis." I gave up and walked in the narrow alley behind the school to avoid seeing the girls in uniforms. I looked down and walked purposefully when I heard a voice say, "Are you looking for a school?" I looked up and saw a lady with blond hair and big, beautiful eyes. I was confused for a moment, but then I nodded my head quickly.

I thought she would take me to the place where I could hear girls running around chasing each other and screaming. But instead, she took me to a green door with a big banner above it with "Khaneh Meher" (the house of kindness) and pushed a buzzer. When I entered, I saw colorful images in the hall and a line of girls and boys. The kind lady placed me at the end of the line and entered an office. The women in the office treated her with respect, saying "Hi, Mrs. Poori, good to see you!" as the blond lady went into a room labeled "Headmaster."

I waited in line, not knowing why. Looking around, I noticed a short, muscular guy staring at me while quietly reporting something to his friends, who laughed nonstop. Feeling uncomfortable and tired of being shy, I asked the girl in front of me, "What is this line for?"

"They told us to wait to be added to the list," said the girl, who had a big mouth.

"What list?" I asked.

"To come here and study." The big mouth smiled until it was her turn to make her way nervously to the room where Mrs. Poori was. As I waited for my turn, I watched three friends chuckling and making fun of everything they saw. Unlike the Iranians, all of us Afghans came to school without a parent. I began to love the people and the place.

The door opened, and the girl came out with an even bigger smile on her face and right away went to the classroom next door. It was my turn.

"Hi again," Mrs. Poori said. "So, tell me about your past education."

I thought and thought. "I can read and write," I said.

"How about math, geography, and science," she said. "Have you studied those subjects?"

I told her yes. The fear of her giving my seat to a student familiar with those subjects made me lie. I understood the mistake I'd made only after I was sent to the room where the girl with the big mouth was. I didn't want to sit next to her, but the only other available seats were on the side with the three loud boys. Reluctantly, I sat next to her. I hoped to find a better spot to be able to focus and do the test.

Soon, the room filled up, and extra chairs were added. Everyone felt as I did—awkward, not knowing anyone and not having anything to say. In the silence, we heard the faint sounds from the girls' school next door. Unlike the other school, we had a mix of boys and girls. Unlike the Iranian students, we had no uniforms; there were about eighty of us in eighty different styles, colors, and types of clothing. We looked so mismatched; some of the students were in work uniforms, and others were in wrinkled clothes.

Shortly after, a man arrived and distributed placement tests. "Remember, if I catch any of you cheating, you will be automatically disqualified, and you will have to wait another year until the next registration," he warned us. He sat and waited for us to finish the test.

After a short time, some students handed in their papers and then waited in their seats, including the girl with the big mouth. I did okay on the reading, but once I got to the math section, I lost my mind; I had no hope of being able to solve anything! The time was moving so fast, and I was still stuck on math. I felt like crying, knowing that I wasn't going to pass, when the girl with the big mouth nervously filled in the empty boxes for me. I wanted to thank her, but it could have put both of us at risk. I smiled at her to show my gratitude.

A few stressful minutes passed until the teacher returned with the papers in his hand and began to read: "Jafar Gholami, you passed. Azita Amini, you passed. Nazif Aziz, you passed. Sori Akbar, you passed."

Suddenly, the girl with the big mouth shouted her excitement, and then her friend did. My heart was sad, but it felt alive again once I heard: "Sonita Alizadeh, you passed."

I couldn't believe it! The big mouth smiled at me again. I was so happy that I forgot to thank her for helping me pass. We were called to form another line for final registration, where I found the opportunity to speak to her.

"You can call me Sori," she said, and her friend added, "I'm Nazif, and your name is Sonita, right?" Nazif's words made me feel warm and included, as I had felt when I first met Ranjita.

Once I received a piece of paper signed by Mrs. Poori, I said goodbye to Nazif and Sori. I left with a huge smile on my face, already planning new lies to tell Nana to secure my return to school the next day—"Latif asked me to come back tomorrow to take care of Fadia." I couldn't wait to get home to share my wonderful day with Zia.

14

School

Early in the morning, I woke up before Nana finished her prayers. I didn't have a backpack, so I put broken pens and pencils I had found in trash bags into a plastic bag. I quietly whispered, "I'm going to see Latif. She asked me to be there in the morning to look after Fadia."

Because I didn't have enough money for the bus, I ran half of the way on foot to catch a busy bus so that I could get a free ride without being noticed by the angry driver. When I arrived at the school, I saw all the faces I'd seen the day before. I felt so wonderful when Sori told me, "We saved you a spot!" Later, I would find out that the school was run by a nongovernmental organization working in Iran to help educate refugee Afghan children.

Then our teacher walked in and said, "I am Miss Saba, your geography teacher. I need your help to learn your names." The beautiful young woman with red lipstick and high heels called our names from a big list in her hands and then, one by one, gave us each a notebook, pen, and geography textbook. I was so excited when she put the book in my hands and immediately flipped through the pages until she called for our attention.

"Okay, let me start with one simple question: What is geography?" she asked, but no one responded, as if everyone was either shy or clueless. At that, Miss Saba began to understand that it was too soon for us to break the ice or to grasp the knowledge we had been deprived of.

Miss Saba was kind. She waited for us to ask questions, and we didn't have to feel guilty about slowing down the lesson. I was one of those who asked a lot of questions, especially when she talked about "north," "south," "east," and "west." I didn't know anything about directions. She tried so hard to help, and in the end, she offered to meet with me after class.

Unlike the mosque in Mashhad, now I had not only reading and writing classes but several, each covering a different, more exciting topic. My favorite class was math. Often, I received awards from my math teacher for completing all my schoolwork on time. "A wonderful student," he said about me, and also about a few other students.

But my excitement about learning had turned me into a liar. And after only a few successful days, Nana discovered my secret. "Don't you understand that your brothers will beat you for leaving the house every week to go to school?" Her loud, agitated voice revealed my secret to my younger brother.

"I'll break your legs if you do that one more time," said Zaher.

For about two weeks, I didn't leave the house for fear of being beaten. Instead, I found more books to read. One of my greatest discoveries was a book of poems by the Sufi poet Hafez. I loved his words: *I wish that I could show you when you are lonely or in darkness the astonishing light of your own being.* Soon after my discovery of poetry, I began to act like Baba, carrying around a book of poetry the same way he had carried a small Quran in his pocket no matter where he went. I enjoyed the work of the poets so much that soon I became one, writing about things that hurt me deeply. I turned my pain into beautifully written lines that even Zia liked. "Oh, this is my favorite," she said, as I read it to her:

> The wind travels through the leaves
> of the pomegranate tree,
> reminding me of a longing
> to be free.
> The birds singing to remind us
> life is not a cage, fly and fly!

Writing made my chest feel light. Playing with words and sentences distracted me from looking at the walls around me.

One day, when I was feeling lonely, I stole bus fare from Nana's purse. I left the house before my brothers woke up and before Nana returned from the mosque. I grabbed my backpack and, without tying my shoelaces, ran until I was far away from the farm. On the bus, I wiped my sweat and prayed for the driver to take me straight to the station without stopping.

The moment the bus stopped at my station, I ran two blocks, stopping when I saw Nazif coming from the other side of the wide alley. The moment we made eye contact, we both ran with our arms open. I felt so strange; I had never done that with anyone, except maybe Fadia and Ranjita. I hugged Nazif tightly.

"Where have you been? You missed so many classes," said Nazif, walking with me to the hall, where we saw Sori. The way she hugged me, I could tell she had noticed my absence too.

The three of us studied together and were rewarded for our

work with a notebook or a pen from our teacher. Some of the students would even ask us for help, especially Ares, who, unlike most of the kids at the NGO school who were thin and shy, stood out as talkative, healthy, short, and goofy. He would jokingly ask me, "Hey Soni,"—he often called me Soni—"do you want to do my homework for me? In return, I can be your boyfriend. Good deal, no?" After each silly statement, his friends would laugh and pat him on the back.

I had missed school, even stupid and goofy Ares. If hugging the opposite sex hadn't been so shameful, I would have hugged him. I could tell he was so happy to see me. "Soni is back! I knew you missed me," Ares said quietly as he made his cool, heavy walk into the class with two friends. All the students made their way to the three classrooms available at the NGO school. At the request of the teacher, I waited by the headmaster's office.

I hadn't shared the reason for my long absence, but Mrs. Poori knew what the problem was. "Do we need to talk to your mom and brothers?" she asked me. This was the main reason many girls had inconsistent attendance at school—their family didn't approve.

"Yes," I said, looking down, trying not to meet her kind eyes. I knew the frequent absences of girls caused her sadness and stress. I was the third or fourth girl who asked her for a visit to help us return to school without facing beatings.

After speaking with Mrs. Poori, I made my way back to class and took out my books, realizing I was far behind. I opened my eyes and ears, despite my head being filled with worries about returning home and seeing Nana and my brothers at the door.

During the break time, Nazif, Sori, and our new friend Hasin played volleyball against Ares and his friends in the small yard. Although we lost, we had so much fun. I watched the clock and took my backpack and left before class had finished.

"Don't disappear. *Mibinamet*," said Nazif, which meant that we would see each other soon.

I ran home, and when I arrived, as I had expected, everyone was awake, wondering where I had gone.

Smack! Zaher slapped me as soon as I entered the yard, yelling, "Didn't I tell you not to leave the house?" The echo of the slap was still ringing in my ears when Nana tried to hit me with her shoe. Fortunately or unfortunately, Latif was there to intervene. But with her there in my home, I couldn't claim that I had been at her place. Instead, I confessed that I had been at school.

"If you do this again, I'll kill you," Zaher threatened angrily. I cried, not because of Zaher's brutal slap but because of everyone's furious reaction to my attending school. Their rage made it clear that I dared not leave the house again unless I wanted to face even harsher punishment.

Zia and Fadia constantly tried to help me feel better, but I found myself angry with everyone, everything, even the walls, the doors, and myself. I wanted to leave the house to get some fresh air away from Zaher and Nana, but I didn't have permission.

One hot afternoon, seated on the carpet with the rest of the family, I received the most unexpected, pleasant guests: Mrs. Poori, with Mrs. Sabor, the therapist at the NGO. My brothers were shocked to receive respected and kind Iranian ladies who cared about us Afghans. Mrs. Poori brought us a bag of all kinds of edible items, which softened Nana's heart, so she welcomed the ladies with pleasure.

My going to school happened because of the magic of Mrs. Poori, who convinced Nana—but not my brothers. That didn't matter, though, because once Nana was convinced, she could lie to my brothers about my absence.

Once I had no fear of Nana, I began to fully pay attention in classes and received top grades. School was a stage for us to be seen and heard. I participated in a poetry competition and won first place. I gave the cash award to Nana. Because money softened Nana's heart, I began to stay out longer to work at the NGO, cleaning classes and bathrooms. That way, I had some money to pay for my bus fare and to purchase school supplies without asking my family.

One day at school, I got caught up and distracted by something wonderful: music. After the last period of school, one of the new teachers took out his guitar and, at the request of the other teachers, agreed to give us a free performance.

The moment he placed his left-hand fingers on different parts of the guitar and his right hand strummed the strings, an amazing, unforgettable melody filled the air. "Wow! How can he do that?" Sori asked me, but I was already lost in the beautiful melody.

After he finished performing, the whole hall filled with loud applause, paying the teacher the respect he deserved for his music. Most students left to go home, but I had to stay to do my job. But first, I waited in the hall for the music teacher, who noticed my eyes on his guitar. "You play so beautifully," I said to him as he stood next to the door, ready to leave as Mrs. Poori walked up to us.

"Oh, this is Sonita," she said, smiling at me. "She's very talented and writes poems!" When the music teacher left, I delayed my work and walked into Mrs. Poori's office.

"Do you think you could ask the man who played the guitar to have a music class for us?" I asked.

"Ha! That would be very fun, but sponsors want us to use this place just for educational topics," she said. "Music can create problems for us because the neighbors do not like refugees. If we are also loud, they would have a good point to file a claim against us."

"But what if we use the basement?" I asked.

"Still a problem, sadly," said Mrs. Poori. But then she took her phone from her purse and said, "Maybe we can do something else." She called someone and then said into the phone: "Mr. Asad, sorry to bother you again, but I have a question. A student of ours, Sonita—you just met her—is very interested in learning music. Do you think you might have any time to donate so she could come and learn?"

I couldn't believe it! When she hung up, she asked me to wait one or two days so Mr. Asad could check his schedule. "He has a wonderful heart," said Mrs. Poori. "I'm sure he'll help you learn music."

I left the office to start cleaning the bathrooms with a big smile on my face.

The next day, I told Nazif, Sori, and Hasin that I might get music lessons. They were super excited for me. "Maybe you could learn to play the guitar and I could read these," said Sori, flipping through the notebook where I wrote all my poems.

That day, our math teacher had to leave early. I convinced my friends to leave with me to go to the nearest mall, where I had seen musical instruments. We were all scared of our brothers finding us wandering around the mall, so we rushed to the basement, where only a few stores were open, teaching music to clients. We laughed and goofed around until my eyes found a beautiful guitar in the far corner of the mall. We walked up to the shop window and looked at all the different instruments. Hasin got excited and wanted to hold the guitar.

We opened the door of the empty store and walked in. To my surprise, I saw Mr. Asad there. "Oh, I think we met yesterday," he said. I was so happy to see him. "I believe you want to learn how to play the guitar, right?"

I said yes with so much confidence. "I can teach for thirty minutes on Mondays," he told me. "Do you have a guitar?"

"No, but I'll buy one."

"Well, I also sell guitars," he said.

"How much is that one?" I asked, pointing to the one that had caught my eye.

"That's a Yamaha. It will be too expensive for you. How about this one?" Mr. Asad took a guitar hanging on his wall and gave it to me. It felt light and beautiful to hold.

"Can I hold it?" Sori asked. She held it, and then passed it to Nazif, then to Hasin in order. I had all the cash I owned in my pocket. I took it out and began to count.

"Sorry, but I don't have enough. Do you have another guitar for about sixty or sixty-five rials?" I asked.

"This would be the only affordable one," he said.

I looked at the guitar again and said, "Maybe I can return next month after I get paid."

Nazif, Sori, and Hasin knew my heart was set on the guitar that I couldn't afford. "How much do you have? I also have five rials," said Nazif, putting the cash she probably saved for her bus fare on top of the money I had saved for months. Hasin and Sori checked their pockets and each contributed whatever they had. I still was short.

"It's okay, pay me back when you can," said Mr. Asad, as

he put the guitar in a black case and gave it to me. The guitar was almost my height.

"Well, since you came to the right place and now have your instrument, I'll give you your first lesson," said Mr. Asad, sketching musical symbols and jotting notes in a music notebook.

"This is a music symbol. This is Do, Re, Mi . . . these are all music notes," said Mr. Asad, asking me to memorize the location of each note on the guitar strings for our next class. I eagerly accepted the lesson and tucked the notebook into my backpack.

"Why aren't you girls learning music?" Mr. Asad asked my friends.

"I would love to learn guitar, but my father thinks music is *haram*," said Sori.

"I'll teach them once I can play," I said. Mr. Asad smiled and wished us good luck.

When we got back to the NGO, we made our way to the basement and opened the guitar case. We all took turns holding the beautiful instrument. I took my notebook, picked a poem, and began hitting the strings just to produce sound as I sang one of my poems. It was one of the short poems and still took several minutes.

I could tell I had bored my friends when I finished the song. "Your poems are too long," Sori said. "A song should be short, and not very sad." This one had been about discrimination against Afghans.

Once it was time to go home, I asked my friends to take the guitar with them because I was too afraid to take it home with me. But they all told me that their fathers wouldn't be happy to see a musical instrument in their home and they would be punished. Since such a punishment was awaiting me if my family found out, I decided to make a safe space for my guitar in the corner of the dark basement next to my cleaning tools.

I knew no one would take it, but even if someone did, it would be better if someone else played it than for me to take it home and see my angry brothers break it. I took my music notebook, and we left school, practicing out loud: Do, Re, Mi . . .

15

Marrying My Dreams

Hatred against Afghans increased in Tehran. The NGO was the only place open to Afghans, but people soon closed it down, breaking its windows and demanding the NGO workers leave the area. We still returned to school, as it was the only thing we had in the whole world.

The NGO survived in the face of discrimination, but my family didn't. One day I returned home to see Nana crying and asking Khaleq, "Where did they take them?" It turned out that Naser, Razeq, and Zaher had been taken away to a refugee camp in a bus. Only Khaleq had managed to open a window and run away.

"There is no way they could have escaped," said Nana, as she put on her hijab. I left with Nana, and we checked a few refugee camps, where we witnessed the humiliation of humanity. There was no place for the people in the camp to even sit down, no food for them to eat, no one to listen to them. I saw a man unconscious on the floor of the basement, and no one helped him.

The last camp we visited was the most challenging, and only those with IDs were allowed inside. I managed to push through and headed straight for the basement, where all the Afghan detainees were kept. I called out for Zaher, Naser, and Razeq, and before long, they rushed to the small window crowded with visitors, tearfully bidding farewell. I was so happy to find them.

"Tell Nana not to give anyone money," Naser warned urgently. "They took our friend's money to release him but then deported him anyway."

I couldn't hold back my tears, seeing them trapped in a place where they couldn't even stretch their legs. Razeq tried to comfort me, saying, "Kokosto, go tell Nana we're okay. We're going home soon. It's not so bad."

His words were meant to reassure me, but they only made me cry harder as I looked at them. How powerless I felt—unable to beg the police officers, like others were doing, to release their family members. We all asked for forgiveness for being Afghans.

Months passed, and I experienced what the therapist at the NGO called depression. I wished I could stay at school forever because home was filled with sadness. But as we girls grew older, even school became a place of sorrow. Sori was forced to marry an old man who had two children; she was only fifteen years old. She attempted suicide, which sickened me emotionally. I wished we could remain children together—still being happy in class and learning together.

My desire to eat or drink was replaced by an overwhelming urge to cry—a feeling that poured out in the poems I wrote at school, on the bus, at home, in the bathroom—wherever I happened to be awake. I cried in private so much, and the only reprieve I found was in writing poetry.

Then Nana decided to return to Afghanistan, taking all of us with her, despite my nightmare of leaving school. My objections to her decision sparked big arguments. "You want to stay here all by yourself? You want to bring shame upon us, just for school?" Nana said as I cried and begged her to let me stay in Iran.

Khaleq also wanted to stay in Iran, but Nana felt he needed someone to take care of him. So Nana relented and gave me permission to stay too—so I could care for Khaleq's needs. This meant I would have to give up school. Nana often prioritized the men in the family over herself and her daughters. I reluctantly agreed. However, as soon as they left for Afghanistan, I broke my promise and returned to the only place that helped my depression: school with my friends. Every day when Khaleq left for work, I would head to the NGO school and then to a nearby gym that I also cleaned, in return for lessons in boxing and karate that helped me release my anger.

I walked around my room quietly, preparing a secret bag. I took my homework out from under my mattress, flipped through the pages, and swiftly put it in the bag. I spent much of my day like this—in hiding. If I were seen in town on my way to school or to work, people might view Khaleq as lazy or dishonorable. No man of dignity would allow his sister to work outside the home to meet her own needs.

For these reasons, I turned our shared bathroom into a library where I did homework. In the afternoons, I sometimes rejected fun games at the NGO school to get home at least an hour before him. After all, like my sisters Latif, Aziz, and Zia, I had learned very well to obey. When I had objections, I would go to the bathroom alone and get them out by crying.

Hard construction work often drained Khaleq's energy, so having me there as his caretaker wasn't a complete waste. But sometimes he threatened to send me back to the rest of the family in Afghanistan. Then, I would cook the most delicious food and clean the house as if dust and bugs were forbidden to be there. Then he'd decide again to let me stay with him.

Now, chuckling to myself, I watched Khaleq disappear into the narrow alley. I quickly ditched the baggy pajamas and long T-shirt that were hiding my school uniform, and I headed downstairs. I couldn't spend the money that Khaleq gave me for groceries and rent on transportation. So sometimes I would do what I used to, sneaking onto a bus if it wasn't filled with guys. If I couldn't do that, I'd run to school.

That morning, I ran halfway and finally succeeded in getting on the bus.

Although I was usually neat and clean when I left the house, the long journey made me sweat and smell like most of the kids at the NGO school. Nazif taught me so many tricks to keep myself looking fresh and neat, but they were of no use when I had to run in the heat.

That day, to my surprise, Nazif arrived at school looking as messy as I did. First I noticed that she seemed sad, and then I saw that her face was bruised. "What happened, Nazif?" I asked, even though I had already guessed the story.

"I told you yesterday that I might come with a bruise on my body," she said.

"At least you made it to school," I said.

"This time I might leave for real." Her sister-in-law, who was her guardian, had come with her to tell Mrs. Poori that it would be Nazif's last day at school.

We all knew this moment was coming. It had happened first to Sori. She had changed so much after her engagement. Among us, she was the one who always had a big smile on her face, but it faded away after that. Sometimes she acted as if she were fifty years old, not fifteen.

"I felt so disgusted when the mullah put my hand in the hand of that man I was supposed to marry," she had told us, crying. "Since then, I hate myself. I wish I could cut off this hand that touched him."

"But he is old," Hasin had said, trying to console Sori. "By the time you are forced to marry him, he might die." Nazif then had held her hands up to the sky, asking God to help us since everyone else was against us—the girls who would give anything to stay in school.

When Sori's father had found her after her suicide attempt, he took her first to a mullah, who told her father to rush her to the hospital. I met them there. When I saw Sori's father in the waiting area, he looked angry. Was it because she hadn't obeyed him, or because she had lied about going to school? Was it because he feared that others would find out what she had done? Was it because of the cost of bringing her back to life?

Her family's response was to give the engagement more time, thinking that maybe, as she grew, she would change her mind.

I hadn't said anything to Sori's father at the hospital. It wouldn't have mattered. It would have been like speaking to a stone.

Now, it was Nazif's turn. I tried to reassure her. "It looks like you fought even harder this time," I said, looking again at her bruised face.

"I did. Still, my brother agreed on the *pishkash*," she said. "Now I have no choice but to do what I told you."

I knew that Nazif's plan to escape her family was as harmful as marrying an old man who already had another wife and kids.

"Don't tell anyone, I know a place where I can go," Nazif whispered in my ear, fearing her sister-in-law would hear her plan.

"Maybe you could meet the guy and act like a crazy girl," I whispered back. "Remember? When you're alone with him, you can laugh and point at the blank walls, mumble nonsense things so he thinks you're out of your mind."

Over the years, me and my friends had invented so many ways to make a guy regret his purchase. One of Sori's favorites was the idea of putting turmeric on your face and coughing as much as you can, then telling the man that you're terribly sick and have only a month to live.

Whenever one of us felt bad, the others would find a distraction like this so that, for just a short moment, we could forget our problems.

"Will I see you soon, Nazif?" I asked.

"Yes," she said, "if my brother doesn't find me and kill me."

Feeling my heart break, I cried quietly. "Ha-ha," Nazif laughed. "When you cry, your nose looks even bigger than it already is." We often joked about our noses. Sometimes it bothered me, but this time, she could make fun of anything—I just wanted her to give me a smile that didn't match her bruised face, one that still looked as if nothing were about to end.

Nazif tried, but deep down in my heart, I knew she was going to be gone like other classmates we knew. Child marriage took all my best friends, and I usually didn't even have the chance to say goodbye to them. I sat by the wall on the ground, looking at Nazif, wishing I could change all of our fates.

"Does it hurt?" I asked her.

"What?"

"Your bruise."

"No," she said. I stayed quiet, as I couldn't look at her

without tears blurring my vision. Then a heavy shadow appeared over my head. "Time to go," said Nazif's sister-in-law.

I hugged Nazif gently, knowing that her delicate body probably had even more bruises under her long black hijab. I cried, as this time she had lost the fight, and I could see her spirit was broken. I knew when she got back home, she would surrender and put all her dreams aside to marry—to be a proper girl, who was young but had to grow up fast to avoid extra beatings.

"Bye, Sonita," said Nazif and closed the door.

The moment she left, I hated her for saying goodbye. We had often said *mibinamet* to each other—see you soon. Now I hated her for not fighting harder, to the death even, as we'd agreed! She'd left school so easily, not even crying. Either she had run out of tears or I had turned crazy, expecting her to fight all of society alone. *She will find a way to escape*, I told myself, hoping it were true.

Seeing her go, I couldn't imagine a different future for myself.

For a few days, the pain of losing Nazif stayed in my heart. Home felt like a prison. I wanted to be at school in case she returned. One morning, I tried to wake Khaleq by making eggs for him. I couldn't go ask him to get out of bed, but I could bang pots, pans, and plates together—and I did. I couldn't bear to miss even a minute of being at the NGO.

Finally, I heard the sound of his favorite singer, Michael Jackson, and I knew it had worked. Khaleq's worldly wealth was a CD player, a small color TV, and one Michael Jackson CD. (At that age, I didn't own anything—not even myself.) Khaleq listened to Michael Jackson more than me. Now, from the kitchen, I wished I were Michael Jackson because then, I thought, my brother would like me.

As Khaleq packed his dusty work bag, he tried the moonwalk here and there. Once his bag was ready, he made his way to the common room, ready to be served. "I made eggs," I said, my eyes daring to look into his. Sometimes he looked so scary that I wished I had never had a brother.

"My job has shifted to another city," Khaleq told me. "It's far from here, but I have a break by the end of each month to come home." Even he knew the sad look on my face was only an act. Because in fact, I felt reborn, knowing I was going to be alone—even if our neighborhood forbade it.

As he began to eat, I held my face still, trying to absorb the excitement of living alone for the first time. Now our neighbors wouldn't see me acting like a thief, hiding behind things until I made sure Khaleq was gone. I could do homework anywhere in the house. I could write poems all day. *Oh!* I thought. I could try the suggestion that someone at the NGO had made: I could put a big sticky note on my wall, so whenever I woke up, I could see the words "I am strong."

I nodded as Khaleq recited all the old rules and a few new ones, as I thought only about how much I could do without him. I could even take a break from cleaning and cooking if I wanted. It all sounded like a dream.

Finally, right after Khaleq left, I arrived at the NGO, and I saw Sori. "Soni, guess what we're doing today?" she asked me.

"Reading and writing?" I guessed.

"No, we're having the Law of Attraction again!"

"Oh nice!" I said with a big smile on my face.

Mrs. Poori had described the Law of Attraction as the idea that whatever you believe in can become the core of your story, and that, if you really work toward your goals, you can achieve them. In other words, "Dreams come true." Hearing that, all the students, both boys and girls, had looked around at each other and laughed. How could she not understand that fate, or God's will, carried out by our families, ultimately determined our story?

"NO! *You* and only you can decide how your life is to be shaped," Mrs. Poori had insisted. Finally, she'd lost her temper, failing to turn us, the nonbelievers, into people who believed in something outside of fate. We'd questioned her so much that I thought she wouldn't hold the class again.

I followed Sori into the classroom, happy to be wrong about "reading and writing."

"Please, take your seats," said Mrs. Poori. The boys hurried to the back of the room, where their laughter and unrelated conversations could go unnoticed by the teacher. The boys' presence, especially Ares's, sometimes made it hard to concentrate. Every day, I had to endure my girlfriends imitating him and repeating his message: "I like you, Sonita, but I deserve better, you know?" Ares loved trying to insult me, now calling me Sony instead of Soni, or sometimes Samsung.

That day, I was Samsung. "Shut the garage," I joked in response, referring to his mouth.

"Sonita!" Mrs. Poori called to me, along with the rest of the class, telling me to sit down and control my voice. Finally, the girls settled on the left and the boys on the right, and the class began.

"Today we will learn how to dream!" exclaimed Mrs. Poori, placing magazines, newspapers, and posters on a desk already filled with notebooks and colored pencils. "In the last class, you all learned that the Law of Attraction means that whatever energy you carry, positive or negative, you will attract.

"The Law of Attraction has three simple steps," she continued, counting them on her fingers. "One, to give your dream a face by finding a picture of it. Two, to believe in your dreams and yourself. And three, the last and most important one, to take action—to take steps to make that dream become a reality."

Met with silence, she continued. "You all know your names, your mothers and fathers, but do you really know yourselves? Do you know about your dreams? What do you know about yourselves?"

"Ha-ha," I giggled to Sori and Hasin, who were seated on either side of me. How silly of her to think we didn't know ourselves.

"Teacher, Sonita has an answer!" Ares couldn't resist the opportunity to appoint me as the class spokesperson against my will. I silently vowed to get back at him.

Mrs. Poori asked me to stand, and I did, initially intending to remain silent. But then, in an attempt to avoid further embarrassment, I blurted out the first thing that came to my mind. "Well, I am Sonita," I said.

"Is that all you know about yourself?" asked Mrs. Poori. I began to sweat, knowing the eyes of the class were on me. How embarrassing, not being able to form a sentence to give her. As the class waited to hear from me, I thought a little more about Mrs. Poori's question.

Finally, I pushed past my silence and said, "I am from Afghanistan."

"What else?" she asked.

"Ummm . . ."

"Can you tell me more about who you *really* are?" Mrs. Poori walked back to the desk and began handing out supplies. "Who is Sonita? Tell me about her. What does she like to eat? What makes Sonita happy or sad? What is Sonita's biggest dream?" Her hands now empty, she held her arms wide for emphasis.

"Biggest dream?" I repeated.

"Yes, what is your biggest dream?"

I didn't want to tell the class my biggest dream—to have an ID card so I could live more freely, like the Iranian children who so often taunted us Afghan refugees. I didn't want to sound too unrealistic. Impossible: none of the kids at the NGO had an ID.

"I want you all to pick a magazine and go through the pages to find pictures of your dreams," said Mrs. Poori.

The class returned to life, and everyone rushed to the desk. "Let me know if you can't find my photo in the magazine," joked Ares from the back of the line. "I'll bring you one to put in your Dreams Book." I laughed, but was more excited to find a picture of my dream.

"Teacher, is this an ID?" One of the kids pointed to a picture in a magazine, and I realized how many kids were flipping swiftly through the pages, looking for the same thing. But despite our shared dream, most of us had never actually seen an ID, or even a picture of one. We only knew that without one, we would never be seen as human in Iran.

When I finally reached the desk, I took one of the magazines. It felt thin; each page had a part already ripped out. I opened it, and suddenly my quest to find an image of my dream led me to dreams I'd never even had. Every page I turned, I found a new dream. "Oh, look at these shoes!" I said to Sori, quickly ripping out the page before someone else could take it. Then I ripped out another one, and another, and then more pages, until my hands could hold no more dreams. I hadn't found my original dream, so on the first page of my Dreams Book, I drew a picture of an ID.

Name: Sonita Jackson
Father: Michael Jackson
Mother: Rihanna
Country: United States
Date of Birth: ?

The first dream I put in my Dreams Book: an ID of my own.

Eventually I chose January 14 as my birthday: the holiday called Sezdeh Bedar. One girl in my class teased me, saying, "No one will celebrate your birthday with you because they will all be rushing to celebrate the first week of the new year"—as if the day she chose for her birthday was any better. But this way, I could imagine that all the people rushing to bakeries and buying flowers and wearing their finest dresses for Sezdeh Bedar were preparing to celebrate my birthday with me.

"But why Sonita Jackson?" asked Mrs. Poori.

"Because I want to live in the United States," I told her,

choosing not to mention that I wanted that musician to be my relative. I knew that so many people—not only Khaleq—liked and respected him.

"The Iranian government won't let you come to Iran if you are from the United States," Mrs. Poori said, laughing. I simply smiled.

"Look at this," Hasin quietly said to Sori and me. She held her notebook under the desk, so no one else could see her dream.

"Wow, he is so cute," Sori commented, seeing the picture of Hasin's dream guy in her Dreams Book.

"Show me yours!" said Sori.

I flipped to the first page of my Dreams Book, then the second, third, fourth, fifth . . . and the twentieth page. I was shocked to learn how many dreams I had in my book and had never said aloud. Looking over the pictures again gave me even more energy. Although I still thought that fate would ultimately drive me in the direction it preferred, I also was intrigued by the idea of making my own future. As unbelievable as it sounded to me, to us, there was so much joy in creating a story that I wished for.

I had given birth to my dreams; I felt like a mother who fell in love with her kids and would do anything to protect them.

Looking at each one of my dreams gave me a feeling of being found. My dreams had become my ID. Now I knew who I wanted to be: I wanted to be independent and have all kinds of shoes and clothes, my own house and my own car. "Sonata"—that was the name of a car I'd found in the magazine, which sounded like my name. And it was nice looking too.

Snip! Snip! The sound of scissors became louder as students hurried to cut out a few last images. Suddenly all these students, who hadn't been able to articulate even one example of a dream, had filled all the pages of their notebooks.

When I left the class to go to the bathroom, I saw Nazif's brother. I stopped for a minute and watched him walk down the hall. There was no need for me to stop him and ask about Nazif; the henna on his hands told me all I needed to know. The poor people in our school spent money on henna only for Eid, engagements, and weddings. *She is gone*, I thought, feeling my head drop.

I returned to the classroom feeling as if I were dead because now I knew that Nazif had failed to run away. Hasin looked over at me, a question in her eyes. I didn't want to tell her about Nazif or remind her that we would likely be sold into a different future.

Hasin and Sori were fighting over pictures. "You're so stupid," I heard Hasin say to Sori, and I thought of our ages—fifteen and sixteen years old. As young as we were, it was exactly the time when we disappeared from school and reappeared in houses filled with children and multiple wives.

I flipped through my Dreams Book and asked myself, "Who is next?"

The ten-year-old Sonita who had been excited about marriage back in Afghanistan felt like a distant memory. That was a little dream. My current, big dreams would require me to marry them—the dreams—work for them, sleep with them, and wake up with them. Marrying a stranger would mean saying goodbye to all the hopes I had just discovered.

"What if we all run away?" I asked Hasin.

"What?" She looked over at me. "What are you talking about?"

"I mean, if we were forced to get married, we could run away," I said, not completely sure of what I meant.

"It's better to get married than to live on the street," said Hasin.

I knew it was a stupid idea: running away from home guaranteed harsh punishment, even death, by your brothers. I looked again at the dreams in my book, wondering what would happen to them when it was my turn.

My best friends and teacher from the NGO in Iran.

As everyone finished their cutting and pasting, I began to write poems in my Dreams Book. I scribbled and then crossed out lines. I felt so broken inside that only screaming on paper could help me calm down. *Poor Nazif*, I thought.

In moments like these, writing made breathing easier.

Finally, everyone left the class, and I was able to get to work. I began my cleaning that day still thinking of Nazif. I also thought of a new dream: a new job. I didn't want to be a cleaner anymore. As I scrubbed the toilets, I made up my mind that when I got home, I would look around for a picture of a lady in a black suit carrying a briefcase. I would paste it into my Dreams Book.

I rushed through the rest of the cleaning and made my way to the gym to begin my second job. When I arrived, the owner of the gym gave me the cleaning supplies. She said she expected me to finish in two hours and then left to go eat. My mind was still racing; I didn't know if I could handle two hours of being locked in a dark basement, cleaning.

I took the broom and began to sweep. In that quiet space, the voices inside my head echoed, reminding me of Nazif's loss, of Sori's turn, of Hasin's and even mine. I wanted to do anything I could to interrupt those voices. I thought about running out into the street, but instead, I put away the broom and walked over to the CD player. I needed some music to distract me!

I plugged in the CD player and put the volume up high enough to take control. "*To jun mani . . .*" I began to lip-sync in Farsi with the familiar song I had heard in the gym before. Then I headed to the bathroom under the stairs to continue cleaning. I scrubbed the bathroom and the mirrors and was about to take out the trash bags when I heard the beginning of a different song. It was rap music; I had heard it before but never was attracted to it.

"*Hshs ajsgkls hsfha!*" The singer sounded like that, or like Michael Jackson—impossible for me to understand. One thing that was clear: his anger projected through his voice and his beat. I dropped the trash bag and listened carefully.

The power of the music lured me over to the speakers. My lips involuntarily opened, and out spilled the poems that I remembered by heart. They sat on the beat nice and tightly, as if they belonged there. The ability to rap made me feel cocky, happy, confident—and extremely powerful.

I knew I was at work; I had to be cleaning. But work could wait. *Maybe I could talk about child marriage and immigration through rap music*, I thought. I knew I could easily forget the powerful new lines that were coming to me, so I rushed to grab a pen and my notebook.

I repeated my old poems and then put some more lines together, just to try my ability to speak as fast as the rapper. I failed, but I succeeded in delivering my whole message without music leaving me behind, as pop music did. I enjoyed every second of the discovery. Exactly when I thought I had no one to speak to, music had spoken to me. Most important, it had enough room for my story.

I listened, sitting on the yoga mats in the gym, and was brought back to the workplace only when I heard the gym's owner return. To be able to find the rapper later, I wrote in my notebook, next to my poems in Farsi, the unfamiliar characters on the CD: E-M-I-N-E-M.

My boss didn't bother to say out loud that she'd noticed the quality of my work decline. We both knew I wasn't at my best. As I set off for my long trip home, the possibility of being fired lingered in my mind. Still, it didn't take away my focus on the new music I'd heard and its possibilities.

Then just as this spark of my dream reignited, I received a call from Latif. "Nana just contacted me," she said. "She's coming to take you back to Afghanistan."

Hearing the words, I gasped and felt confused and exposed—like a soldier being thrown into the battlefield without any means of defense. I felt my breath catch again as my mind played tricks on me, whispering, "Your turn."

16

Finding My Voice

I walked into a film and music store that had a long line of people. I had been waiting for only a few minutes when the shop owner noticed my discomfort among the male customers, being the only female there. "How can I help you, Miss?" he asked, holding the other customers back.

"Do you know this rapper?" I showed him the name: Eminem.

"Of course! Do you want his music?" he replied.

"Yes!"

"How many gigabytes is your SD card?"

"I've deleted everything on it, so it has plenty of space."

"Do you speak English?"

"No."

"I promise, even if you could speak English, you still wouldn't understand what this guy Eminem says. He's famous for not being understood." The shop owner laughed. The moment I left the shop, with so much excitement, I put my headphones on and played . . .

OH MY GOD! Can he be real? Can someone talk that fast? I wondered. Each track awoke a new feeling in me.

I listened to his music again and again. After that day, I became the music seller's permanent customer. I asked him to sell me a few beats and give me a discount, as I had become a regular. He considered my situation and listened to my feelings carefully.

"So you want a beat to rap about child labor? Something sad?" he asked.

"Yes, that's right," I responded.

"Okay, here you go. I uploaded a few to your SD card," he said, shocking me with the speed of his work.

"How do you do that? Where do you get all these songs?" I asked.

"From YouTube," he replied.

"What's YouTube?" I asked, not understanding anything he said.

When I arrived at the NGO, I impatiently waited for our break to perform my first rap song for Sori and Hasin. Once we got to the basement, where we did all our forbidden activities, I took my broken phone, played the beat, and began to rap. It felt so wonderful. I was so drowned in my performance that only when the beat was over did I look around to see so many of the kids around us clapping after I closed my notebook.

Omid, Ares's friend, was among the uninvited audience. He was such a nice guy, polite and always offering to help me with cleaning or carrying things. He also wrote poems whenever he could. "You're amazing, Sonita!" said Omid, making me feel even more shy.

"WOW, Sonita," Sori said, still clapping. "You should go on the TV show *Afghan Talent*."

"Ha! Being on TV is a good way to convince her brothers to kill her and end her dream of becoming a rapper, dummy Sori," Hasin said, laughing at Sori's impossible suggestion.

"Can I do it?" Sori asked. I played the beat, and she took

my lyrics and began to do something that she thought was rap, but she struggled to catch the beat. We all laughed. The fun of music encouraged Omid to share his rap song with us. There was something about rap music that united all of us.

Once our break was over, I asked Omid if he knew of any place where I could record my song. He mentioned one, and the next day, I left after school to find it. I was afraid of everything around me—of people who didn't like Afghans, of crowded areas where I might see Khaleq, and of my backpack that was full of lyrics written against the Iranian government and the treatment of Afghans. Carrying my backpack felt like I was carrying drugs. If I had been caught by the police, I would have received a drug dealer's sentence. Music, especially political rap, was banned in Iran.

I appeared calm and walked peacefully, as Omid had suggested, because illegal recording activities had been reported by others. I didn't want to cause trouble for the guy who had agreed to record my song. I spotted Omid near the Blue Mosque, and he asked, "Are you ready?" Feeling a mix of excitement and nerves, I followed as he led the way.

We entered a five-story building. A man about Razeq's age greeted us in the basement. "Welcome guys, this way." Inside was a small room with a tiny booth where I saw a microphone. The studio walls were covered with egg boxes to prevent sound leaking outside. There was a small desk with a computer on it, and the room was lit with warm, blue light.

"I'm Soud," said the music guy. "Tell me: When did you start rapping?"

"A few days ago."

"Oh cool, do you want to give me the beat?" He uploaded the beat onto software I couldn't even begin to comprehend.

After we bargained on the right price, he got busy preparing for my session.

I entered the booth. After adjusting the microphone level, he put a thin, black sock on the pop filter to reduce unwanted sounds. He handed me a pair of headphones and left the small booth. I was so excited; my voice sounded so clean. *This is legit!* I thought. I had practiced my lyrics at least a hundred times before stepping into the studio. When I heard the beat, I effortlessly spat out clear and complete words that didn't require any retakes.

"Honestly, I'm shocked," Soud said. "Among my sixty-five clients, there are only two other female rappers, and you stand out as exceptionally on top of your work. Nice job!" Hearing this made me feel so amazing. Since we had enough time, Soud cleaned the track right away and uploaded it to my SD card.

"Where do you plan to release it?" he asked. I assured him that I would be sharing it only with friends. "Cool, just don't credit me because I have no money or energy to deal with the police," he said.

After the recording, I went with Omid back to the music shop and requested a few films. Omid helped me borrow his friend's laptop, and I began to learn how to edit music videos. I copied clips of several movies about war, poverty, and children, and I pasted the films into the software, making hundreds of cuts and mixing them until I created a music video. Once it was done, I watched it over and over, admiring my work, impatient to share it with my friends at school.

Finally, the day arrived: the release of my first rap song! "Close the door," I told my friends and the other students, as new and old fans pushed into the basement. I hit the play button on the computer, and the sound of music and the images took over. I looked at my friends, so invested in my words—in the story I managed to tell through film clips.

After the song was over, several students said, "That is so powerful!"

"Why don't you have your name on the clip, or your picture?" a girl asked. I told her I had to do music secretly so my family didn't know; there was no way I could be in the video. She understood very well.

Once I gained confidence from the students, I found the courage to share the song with Mrs. Poori. To my surprise, she cried when she saw it. Then she congratulated me for awakening in her a deeper desire to continue helping Afghan kids. "Your words are powerful, so touching. Can I share it with my friend Rokhsareh?"

It was a life-changing moment for me; I must have been good if she wanted to share it with her friend. "Yes, please share it with more people," I said.

"You speak so beautifully about Afghan kids feeling like they don't exist without an ID and Iranian kids not wanting to be friends with Afghan kids," said Mrs. Poori as she gave me a long hug. Her embrace made me feel the way music did—calm, safe, free.

I was in class one day doing math with Sori when Mrs. Poori asked me to her office. I walked in and saw a beautiful lady with red hair, red shoes, and a red scarf worn halfway. I could tell her favorite color was red.

"Sonita, meet my friend Rokhsareh," said Mrs. Poori. I said hello, feeling awkward and avoiding her eyes.

"You have a beautiful name. What does it mean?" Rokhsareh asked.

"I don't know," I responded.

"I heard your rap song. It's very touching. I'm a director; I direct films."

"I'll leave you two to talk," Mrs. Poori said. "Come, sit here, Sonita." I sat on her soft chair, and then she left the room.

"The reason I'm here is to learn what gave you the courage to start rapping," Rokhsareh said.

I didn't know how to answer her. I thought, *I don't need courage to rap, I just need a beat.* There wasn't just one thing that gave me courage, and it didn't "just happen." To give her an honest response, I had to recount the many challenges I had faced until then—challenges that strengthened me, each in a different way: when I was a little girl playing outside where only boys could play; when I was constantly called a dirty Afghan in Iran and still went door to door asking to be accepted in school.

I decided that I didn't have courage; I had determination. Or if I were to describe it in a better way, I ignored my fear of failure because my dreams were far more powerful than the police or the people around me. Thanks to Mrs. Poori, my dreams fed me hope.

"I had lived my entire life in fear, and I saw that fear always kept me chained," I told Rokhsareh, who seemed captivated by my story. "In order to be free, I had to let go of my fear first. That was all!"

"Well, you used some very famous movies in your clip, without permission. But if you'd like, I can help you with your next music video."

When Rokhsareh said that, I forgot to be reserved and began to question her until it was time for her to go. "You continue your work; I'll come help you after my trip to Europe," said Rokhsareh. I was amazed to know that she had been to Europe, where women aren't banned from making music.

As days went by, I slowly began to believe that I wouldn't see Rokhsareh again. But then she returned, this time with a big camera. From that day on, I saw her every single day. She asked me dozens of questions. "I want to make a documentary about you," she said.

"Like a movie?" I asked.

"Yes, about you, rap music, and being an Afghan refugee in Iran."

"Do you think people would watch it?"

"Definitely. People in Europe and America will see it," she said. I was thrilled by the idea of being seen and heard in different countries that we had only heard of in our geography class.

"Oh, by the way, I found out the meaning of your name," said Rokhsareh. "It means a swallow bird. A very cool meaning, and it fits you. You have always been migrating, like swallows do."

"A swallow bird, cool! Thanks!" I said to Rokhsareh, as she prepared her camera to start documenting my life.

Sori and Hasin always shied away from the camera and the team that Rokhsareh sometimes brought with her, but I loved the experience of being in front of a camera, speaking about my past and future. With Rokhsareh, I had a permanent listener, and, for the first time, I felt like my story mattered. Unlike my family, she gave me the chance to speak and share my feelings without being interrupted.

"You know, I like making rap songs," I told her. "I feel like with music no one can interrupt me." Right away, she turned her camera on and asked me to expand on what I had just said. Rokhsareh believed that every part of my life was worth sharing. She was like Mrs. Poori, so caring and attentive to details. Even though I wasn't allowed to be in front of a camera, to speak about the limitations my family and society imposed on me, I was tired of living just to satisfy others. I wanted to talk to Rokhsareh and her camera. I wanted to be noticed!

One day, after recording my new song "Election," Rokhsareh decided to stay longer with me at my place. To my surprise, Khaleq walked in while we were discussing sending my song to a music competition in Afghanistan.

"Hi, I'm Rokhsareh," she said, standing respectfully as Khaleq placed his hand on his chest in return. Rokhsareh invited Khaleq to join us for tea and to answer his questions, which of course arose when he saw a large camera in our home.

"I'm a filmmaker; I carry my camera everywhere with me," said Rokhsareh, trying to help Khaleq relax. "How do you feel about the upcoming elections in Afghanistan?" she asked him.

"Election?" Khaleq asked. "I wasn't aware of it. Plus, whether there's an election or not won't really make a difference."

"Why not? If people choose the right person, then you could return to Afghanistan," Rokhsareh said. "Don't you want that?"

"I don't really know. I feel like I don't belong anywhere," Khaleq said. "In Afghanistan, we run for food, and in Iran, we run away from the police. I don't know if I miss any of that."

"I understand. This is happening in Afghanistan and Iran because of the lack of a true leader."

Rokhsareh and Khaleq continued their conversation, which made me happy. Although Khaleq and I had never had even a five-minute conversation, he was comfortable with Rokhsareh, whom he had just met.

The next day, I was at Rokhsareh's beautiful apartment. I had to upload my song for the music competition. I was super nervous, knowing that all the rappers from Afghanistan were invited to submit a song about the importance of people participating in elections.

"It's okay," I told Rokhsareh while reading the names of other rappers I had never heard of before. "Even if I lose, it's important that I try." I never thought Afghanistan had so many rappers; I always assumed that rap was a foreign practice that many traditional Afghans, who prefer to stick with old, undeveloped customs, would not welcome.

"Afghans are changing," said Rokhsareh, noticing my surprise. "They would never have a competition for rap music if they weren't in favor of it."

I usually enjoyed competitions, but this time it took all of my patience. Rokhsareh and I waited anxiously for news from the judges. The moment Rokhsareh had her laptop, she set up her camera, put a mic on my shirt, pressed record, and sat next to me. "Are you ready to hear the final results?" she asked, knowing I was dying to find out.

Rokhsareh opened her email and clicked on a Skype link. She began speaking with a man named Travis, who greeted her with a big smile. They talked for a few minutes in English, and then I interrupted Rokhsareh and asked her to translate for me.

Then the moment finally came. "Okay, Sonita, they made a final decision," said Rokhsareh.

"And???" I asked, desperate to find out the results before my heart stopped from too much anxiety.

"About sixty rappers wrote a song about the elections."

"And?"

"And you won! You won a thousand dollars!"

I felt like I was lifted into the sky. "You won"—this short phrase—filled me with unbelievable happiness. I didn't know how much a thousand dollars was in Iranian money, but I felt like I had won a million rial. My song was making its way into the ears of so many people, whether or not they wanted to hear me.

I felt so close to my biggest dream: becoming a famous rapper known by everyone in Afghanistan. I didn't keep this image just in my Dreams Book; I practiced it in real life. When we had the chance, Sori and Hasin would help me stage a scene where I was invited to major TV programs and interviewed about how I became a great rapper.

Before receiving the money, I planned to give it to Nana. I hoped that a thousand dollars would be enough to buy my freedom so I could belong to myself and live with music forever.

When I returned to school after the weekend, a girl exclaimed, "Oh my god! I saw you on TV last night!"

"Me too!" another girl added.

"I was on TV?" I asked, feeling both scared and happy.

"I told my father you're my classmate," said the first girl, proudly looking at me.

"Soni!!!" Hasin screamed. "I heard you were on TV—Tolo TV, the biggest one in Afghanistan! Did you see it?" I said no, explaining that I didn't have cable TV to see my first appearance on Afghan television.

A few unbelievable days passed. I was lucky that my family hadn't seen my song on TV; otherwise, Nana would have called me about the shame I had brought to the family. The fear of negative responses from my family forced me to pray for their well-being every day, yet I still didn't want to speak to or see them. They wanted me to follow the crowd, but I wanted to follow my dreams. I didn't want us to upset one another by fighting over our differences.

I felt so happy and safe with Rokhsareh that I preferred to be at her apartment whenever I could, even though I had my own space free from my bossy brothers. Whenever I had the chance to hang out with her, I would take my Dreams Book with me because, after Mrs. Poori, she was the one who truly believed in the notebook filled with images that I had promised myself to turn into realities. Rokhsareh had become my source of strength.

"Do you want to see the palace I dream of studying in?" I asked Rokhsareh, as she was making food for both of us and her friend, Roham, a kind man who donated time to teach me guitar. "Yes, show me!" Rokhsareh responded and was amazed to see such a beautiful sight.

"Do you think there is such a place to have all kinds of musical instruments all in one place?" I asked.

"Of course. Music schools in other countries are even better than this."

"Are you serious?"

"I am," she said. "Maybe one day you'll see it!"

Although I was a person who could imagine any crazy thing, the idea of ending up in a different country to study music seemed too unbelievable. It wasn't a dream; it sounded like an impossible life. It sounded so much like heaven that only dying would get me there, I thought.

A few weeks after the release of my song, I received news: "Nana will arrive in Tehran tomorrow," said Latif, who was more in touch with Nana than I was. My heart, filled with hope, suddenly felt so weak and afraid of the unknown future Nana had dreamed for me. I had missed her so much, I had missed everyone, but seeing her meant letting go of school, friends, and music. I was happy at the thought of seeing Nana again, but I imagined she would take me back to Afghanistan. At least that's what I told Rokhsareh, who appeared to be even more concerned for me.

17

Daughters for Sale

When I saw Nana at the bus terminal, I ran to give her a big hug. How wonderful it was to smell her familiar scent and see her face with a big smile covered by her tears. Rokhsareh managed to film a little, even though she feared Nana's reaction.

"What is the camera for?" Nana asked.

"She makes short films, just for herself," I said as Nana tightened her hijab, shying away from the camera. Nana gave Rokhsareh a hug too, and then I carried her suitcase to the bus that would take us to where I lived.

It turned out I had been right. One day, as her travel visa was close to expiring, Nana announced her reason for visiting me: "I need you to complete all your work before next Monday. You are coming home to Afghanistan with me." Her statement left me shattered.

I didn't say much, as she was already unhappy with me for having a guitar at home. "If your uncle finds out you're learning music instead of doing house duties, they will cut all contact with us," she had said, showing no interest when I told her I had won a music competition and had money to help us. Nana's indifference to music persisted even when Rokhsareh carefully told her about my talent in writing lyrics about issues we all dealt with.

Nana remained cold, demanding I return with her. Rokhsareh decided to stay quiet. "Maybe you could give Sonita a little bit more time, Nana," said Latif, while brushing Fadia's hair.

"Her future husband will not wait for her," Nana added.

Husband?! Images of Nafiz and Sori went through my head. I was about to become like them—sold to a man!

Hopelessness and agitation found me, locked in a dark room with my two greatest weapons: my Dreams Book and my poetry notebook. I looked at my Dreams Book and thought, *How stupid of me to think I could have a different future.*

I looked at my trembling hands and hurried to the bathroom, splashing cold water on my face to regain my senses. As water dripped down my face, I stared at my reflection in the mirror, telling myself, *I want to be a rapper, not a bride!*

When Rokhsareh didn't find me at school, she came to our home. "Can you buy me?" I asked, as she was holding her camera, documenting the end of my dreams.

"What do you mean?" she asked.

"My mother wants to take me to Afghanistan to sell me to a guy so they can purchase a wife for my brother. If you pay my mother nine thousand dollars, I promise to pay you back once I have a concert," I spoke quietly, so my mother couldn't hear my words through the thin walls.

Rokhsareh took her eyes from mine, indicating her lack of power to change the life of her protagonist. "Sonita Jan, I am here to make a documentary of you, a refugee girl who raps in Iran where music by and for women is banned. If I interfere with your life, it puts my work into question, and it would no longer be a documentary. My two years of work would be wasted too."

Hearing this from the person who initially believed in my music, in my dreams, was a knife to my heart. I said nothing and stared at the ground, angry with Rokhsareh, angry with my family, and hating myself for being so powerless.

Rokhsareh quit filming, seeing my persistent silence. She took the microphones off of me and walked to the common room, thinking that talking to Nana one more time could change her mind. "Sonita is a good musician and an excellent student, her teachers told me," said Rokhsareh, hoping to reach a solution.

"The qualities that she holds are equivalent to shame," Nana said. "Her brothers and her uncle would be very angry to learn that she intends to engage in something that is *haram* and adds no value to her household qualities."

"I have so many big dreams," I yelled from the other room.

"Your sisters were dreamers too, but now they have children," said Nana, challenging the use of my dreams to justify my wish to escape marriage—a must for every girl I knew. When Rokhsareh understood Nana's strong determination to take me to Afghanistan to my buyer, she left.

"Nana, one day I can become so rich, I could buy us a house, gold earrings for you and Zia," I said. "I could probably even take us to a different, better country."

"What if you let her finish school and then marry her off so she won't be illiterate like the rest of us?" asked Latif, as she inhaled hookah smoke.

"For Afghans, education does more harm than good. If the

guy knows she has been in an NGO mixed with boys, her value will decrease," said Nana.

"But her virginity will prove that she has never been with any boys, and he will never know about the NGO," said Latif. "Sixteen is the right age for marriage. Waiting for her to finish her studies will not do us any good."

I heard several different reasons from Latif, and one word from Nana: NO! I felt like crying, screaming, but I willed myself to avoid completely breaking down. "She has to go with me," Nana said. "Sonita, do your last business with the school, as I said."

I sat in the corner of the room, speaking to my Dreams Book: "I know you could not be as true as Mrs. Poori said." I looked at each page. Tears welled up from my eyes, leaving a mark on every one of those pages.

"Nana, look at this, this is the map to my future." I showed my Dreams Book to her.

"I don't recall if I ever had any dreams," said Nana, closing the book and handing it back to me. "Look at me, I still survived."

I opened it again. "Look at this, I want to help you fix your teeth and get Botox when I am financially stable," I said to Nana. She didn't even look at the page. She behaved as if I were an annoying child who couldn't keep quiet. I didn't blame her for not caring that while she was busy enduring war and poverty, wrinkles appeared on her forehead before their expected time. Nana's primary goal was survival, not maintaining her appearance.

I knew Nana had a hard life. I wanted to give her the happiness that was taken from her, but she would only be satisfied with my sale. "What are these tears for?" she asked. "You are no different from your sisters, who married the men we suggested. Or perhaps you are in love with one of the boys from the NGO?"

Nana's question made me feel like a traitor. My tears were about the loss of my future.

I knew Nana loved me so much. *What is happening to you, Nana*? I asked myself. *Why are you acting so cruel? Please don't make me hate you, because I love loving you.* With so many mixed thoughts and emotions, I felt my faith in my dreams declining. I needed space, but I had none. So I put the Dreams Book aside and asked Nana, "When do we leave?"

"In four days."

"Then I have to see my friends at the NGO to say goodbye to them."

Nana said nothing in response. Maybe she was so shocked by how easily I gave up my fight. Once Nana and Latif began drinking tea and discussing Latif's life, I walked to the clock on the wall and turned it back by two hours, ensuring that Nana wouldn't question me if I returned late, after the NGO had closed.

I took my backpack filled with books and poems and ran in the opposite direction from the NGO. I had about four hours to find myself. I called Sori, but got no answer. She was probably in the middle of her class, which was mine too, before Nana came to Iran.

As I walked through crowds, I bumped into people. Where was I going? What was I looking for? I slowed down and began breathing normally. I ended up in a new neighborhood, so much better than ours. It had a small park where the elders were busy reading *Hamshahri*, the newspaper where we had found pictures of our dreams.

The presence of several people in the park made me feel safe, so I sat on a bench. Behind me was the kids' playground. I heard them screaming and running around with big smiles on their fresh faces, while their mothers chatted. One of them was feeding a newborn. Was that going to be me soon? I wondered. Was she also forced into marriage? Could I ask them for advice? I still struggled to believe that I soon would be owned by someone.

I thought of the question Mrs. Poori had asked all the students in the Law of Attraction class: "You have two types of future: one that your society will design for you with its own interests, and one that YOU create for yourself. Which one do you choose?"

I couldn't recall how I had responded in class, but now I was sure of the answer. I wanted a future of my own, even if it meant sacrificing my life. Sitting alone on the bench, with a little space to hear my thoughts, I understood that I could live without a family to support me. However, without a purpose, my life would not excite me for even a moment.

What would be the reason to live like Nana, Latif, and Aziz, without music, without dreams? Slowly, I began to feel better, realizing that deep down, I was still the confident Sonita who believed in herself and her dreams. I wanted to be worth more than my price tag of nine thousand dollars. I wanted to become so precious that no one would dare to ask for my price.

After about two hours wandering in the park, I took my backpack and walked fast to the NGO before it closed. I arrived and knocked on Mrs. Poori's office door.

"Come in," she said. She looked happy to see me. "I was getting worried about you. Is it true that your mom is going to take you to Afghanistan?" I nodded as I sat down in her chair.

"What can you do to persuade your mother to let you stay here?"

"Wish I knew. She wants to sell me into marriage because my brother wants to be able to pay for a wife," I said.

Mrs. Poori gave me several reasons to fight my mother's wish. "You are so talented, don't let anyone, not even your family, tell you differently," she said. Her words gave me more hope and energy to fight for my future.

"I really hope you can talk to my mother," I said. "Maybe you and Rokhsareh could lend me some money to give to her?" I asked nervously, knowing that Rokhsareh had rejected such a request earlier.

"We can't do that, Sonita. We have so many kids in need. The money we receive from people is to pay for your education, nothing more," said Mrs. Poori, looking upset. "I know you are a strong girl. Don't let anyone sell you a different future." She was so happy and encouraging, like a person giving life to the dead.

"I still have my own future, which you saw in my Dreams Book," I said.

"*Afarin beh to*," she said, proud of my determination.

Although I had always dreamed of hearing those words—I'm proud of you—from Nana, hearing it from Mrs. Poori came close. "I heard your rap song," she added, "and I really like it." I looked at her with a big smile, seeing a candle burning in the darkness that had occupied my mind. I didn't have only four or five fans who were fourteen and younger; I now had two significant fans, Rokhsareh and Mrs. Poori.

"Is there any chance you and Rokhsareh could speak with my mother again?" I asked Mrs. Poori. She gave me a long, nice hug, which I needed, and accepted my request.

Early in the morning I arrived at the NGO with Nana. I had

lied to her, saying, "I need you to come with me to the NGO to talk to Mrs. Poori because she has shown interest in making a deal with you." I made my way to Mrs. Poori's office, where Rokhsareh and her crew were busy preparing the camera for a final conversation between Rokhsareh and Mrs. Poori. I didn't tell them that Nana was expecting to get some money from them until she entered the office.

I felt bad seeing Mrs. Poori feeling upset with Nana, but I could understand why. I looked at Rokhsareh and Mrs. Poori. They both seemed tired of their unsuccessful negotiations with Nana.

Rokhsareh was seated in the back of the room. The cameraman focused on Nana, who was sitting by the door, facing Mrs. Poori. My heart was rising to my throat. I couldn't sit there, watching Nana bargaining on my price, so I left the office, and I felt better when I saw Sori in the yard.

"You didn't respond to my text last night. What's your plan now?" she asked.

"In just a few minutes I'm going to have a better idea, once my mother is done speaking with Mrs. Poori and Rokhsareh." Then I turned off the microphone attached to my hijab and I began to complain. "I thought Rokhsareh was my savior. Now she's probably happy that my life is about to end—this will probably make her documentary even more interesting. I'm struggling to survive, and she still cares about her stupid filming. I wish she could pay my mother."

"Have you seen a picture of the guy they want you to marry?" Sori asked.

"No, and I hope I will never see him. One thing I'm sure of is that he's not going to see me either. I'll run away if that's my last option."

"Or you could make him not want you," Sori reminded me. Whenever I felt bad, Nazif and Sori both distracted me so well.

We were still in the middle of brainstorming ideas when Rokhsareh walked into the yard with a grim face. I was thinking about other options when she gave me the greatest news ever: "We will pay your mother two thousand dollars, and in return, you can stay in Iran for six more months. This will give you time to finish school and some of your songs."

"Really? *Teshakor khanom*! Thank you!" I thanked Rokhsareh nonstop. I wanted to cry; my heart was filled with joy and hope once again. Although Rokhsareh was unhappy that her money could purchase me for only six months, I thought it was enough to buy my freedom and prove to my family that I was worth more than the price tag they had put on me.

Nana left Iran, not knowing that she cast a big shadow of fear over me. I dreaded that the six months might slip away without my finding a way out of the planned marriage. But then, before I could step into six months of independence, I heard the terrifying news. "A police officer came to the NGO asking for you," said Mrs. Poori.

"Did he say why?"

"Your music," she said. "You're breaking the laws and making protest songs."

"How could they even have access to my songs?"

"People who don't like you, or the work we do, have definitely found a good reason to report us," Mrs. Poori said.

"What does this mean?" I asked, as my heart tumbled.

"Sonita, I love you like my own child, but to keep this place open for other children, I have no choice but to ask you to leave for your safety and for the sake of your friends who have no place but the NGO."

I could have walked away before Mrs. Poori had to beg me to leave, but I needed one more moment in the place I had thought would embrace me for six more months.

Hasin and Sori both encouraged me, telling me not to let sadness overwhelm me, even though they appeared sadder than I looked. I took a look at the most valuable assets of my life, my friends, and I offered them a sad goodbye.

Without school, I'd also lose the cleaning job that helped me pay my expenses. Before being completely paralyzed by the challenges I faced, I reminded myself why I had asked Nana for time: to move forward with school and music. And although school was gone, no matter what, I still had music.

I still felt fortunate that despite being denied education and the chance to see people I loved, Rokhsareh was still there for me. She cared deeply and tried to help me navigate the fear and uncertainty of a future that seemed to offer only two possibilities: becoming a bride or a rapper.

The thought of being in a wedding dress haunted me day and night, but I was able to manage it once I started writing music again. I channeled my fear and anger into a song titled "Daughters for Sale." I wrote it for Nana, my brothers, and my friends' families, urging them to consider our feelings before selling us girls into marriage.

Let me whisper to you all of my words
So no one hears I speak of the selling of girls
Everyone says no one should listen to our voice
The tradition of the world—women have no choice

Scream from the suffering of a lifetime of silence
Scream from traumatic wounds, a body in defiance
Scream for a body that's exhausted in its cage
Broken by price tags that come with young age

"I really feel the pain in these words," Rokhsareh said after hearing the song. "I'm sure it will reach your mother."

"I want the music video to show me in a wedding dress with bruises on my face," I told her. She took notes while I described the scene I envisioned for Nazif. I always imagined her in a wedding dress, with bruises on her face that makeup couldn't fully conceal.

Rokhsareh agreed with my vision and added more details. Her approval meant the world to me. She respected the story I had conveyed so much that within just a week, she helped me create a music video for it.

Finally, it was ready—my ultimate shot to escape marriage. Then Rokhsareh showed me how people would be able to see my video. "This is called YouTube," she said. "People will watch your song here. Are you ready to be heard?"

"Wow, this is YouTube?" I asked. I always thought YouTube was a big store, like a mall. "Who sees it?"

"Anyone can see it."

I knew that with only six months left, I had no choice but to risk more and appear on YouTube without a full hijab and in a wedding dress. People in Afghanistan often thought movies were real; seeing me in a wedding dress probably would make them think that I was real. But for sure my value as a wife was going to drop, and a potential suitor might consider someone else more suitable.

I thought it was a great risk, but one that had no downside.

I would win either way. "I'm ready!" I said with confidence, and the song was out!

I had no access to YouTube, but Rokhsareh called me in the morning to say that my song had gone viral. "Viral?" I asked, not knowing what that meant.

I met her at her apartment, and she typed "Daughters for Sale" in her computer, and the results appeared on the screen. Rokhsareh pointed to the number of views. "Look at how many people have commented!" she said. "The best part is that they agree with you!"

I was confused: I had grown up in a family and a society where few people, other than my friends, supported what I said. Do people really support me? I kept wondering this as Rokhsareh read each comment.

"So good," she read and translated comments that were in English. I was shocked to see that even people who didn't understand my language had heard my song. If people in other countries had heard it, did that mean Nana and my brothers had too?

No matter how hard I tried to convince myself that I had to take the risk in order to be heard, I still feared Nana and my brothers calling to shame me for what I had done. I was so afraid that I left home to stay at Rokhsareh's place while she was traveling.

I turned off my phone, which meant disregarding all the wonderful messages I received every day. Friends told me all the places they accidentally heard my new song and about girls on *Afghan Talent* performing "Daughters for Sale" and advancing to the next level of competition. I thought not having my phone would help reduce my stress, but the voices in my head still shouted that I would be punished for what I had done.

I tried to distract myself with cooking. I took out a bag of frozen meat, and while carelessly trying to cut it, I accidentally stabbed my left hand with the knife. The sudden sharp pain snapped me back to reality. I sat down as blood spread across the white, uncarpeted floor. As my wound opened, allowing more blood to leave my weakened body, I felt no pain, only an overwhelming sleepiness. I wrapped a kitchen cloth around my hand and pressed it hard, but blood still leaked out. I lay down on the floor, and after a moment, I forced myself to get to my phone, turn it on, and call for help.

My Afghan friend Lima, a kind older lady whom I knew through Rokhsareh, lived nearby. She took me to the hospital where my wound was treated. I returned home to sleep so I could regain my strength, but then I received the call that caused so much fear and distraction. "Home"—the word appeared on my phone, daring me to look at it. After several rings, I picked it up.

"Salaam," I said in a tired voice, ready to be blamed for a crime.

"Sonita, how are you?" asked Nana, in a less angry voice. Was my song the reason she was calling?

"I'm good, Nana. How are you and Zia?"

"We're okay. I saw your song on Tolo TV. It was good."

When Nana said this, I was reborn. My loss of blood forgotten, I gained so much strength just from hearing Nana say, "It was good." To me, this meant the song was spectacular!

"What did you see?" I asked her with so much excitement.

"I saw you in a wedding dress. It was good that your hair was covered." This was probably the longest conversation that Nana and I had ever had on the phone. I imagined my song touched her heart.

"Sonita, it was so funny when your song appeared on TV.

We were all about to eat dinner, and there was your face on the screen!" said Zia, laughing.

"Tell me more about it! Who was home?" I asked, eager to hear the details that made me feel loved and heard.

"We were all in the guest room with our guests, about to serve dinner, when I saw you on TV and screamed, 'Sonita is on TV!'" Zia continued. "Nana, Razeq, and our guest ran to the living room. It was so funny!" I noted every single detail about my family seeing and hearing my song.

"Did Razeq or Naser say anything?" I asked, worried that I still might not have gained my brothers' support. "Only Razeq has seen it. He smiled. I think he likes the song. At first, he and Nana both thought your bruises were real," said Zia.

After the call ended, I took a moment to reflect on the conversation. I still couldn't believe that Nana thought my song was good. I wasn't confident that my brothers would feel exactly how she did, but if my mother was on my side, I thought convincing my brothers could be a little easier. I felt so great. I put a blanket over myself and lay down on Rokhsareh's sofa to sleep.

18

The Other Side of the World

Rokhsareh returned from her trip overseas with news. "BBC News wants to interview you," she said, mentioning a message she'd picked up through my YouTube channel that she had created for me.

"BBC?" I asked, surprised. I had always heard of the BBC as one of the greatest news channels, and now I was going to be speaking with them?

I felt nervous speaking with a reporter, knowing that so many people would be watching and listening. Still, I took advantage of the opportunity to share my story and the fate of my friends. I got better at interviews, as I did several others with popular international channels. It wasn't surprising to me that most of the interest was from English speakers; such a tale was fresh and new for them. Afghan programs were mainly interested in my music since my story was quite common in Afghanistan.

Two weeks passed, and Rokhsareh received a growing number of interview requests and emails. One stood out, prompting her to connect with a person named Cori Stern. She'd mentioned her to me.

"We have to speak to this lady who saw your song and is

a fan!" she said, as she opened her computer and logged into Skype. After a few seconds, a lady with blond hair, a beautiful smile, and no scarf appeared on the screen. "Hi, *hahajdhfgsfh dhfhskshf*," she said—I only understood "Hi."

Rokhsareh and Cori chatted extensively while Rokhsareh's camera captured it all—including my amusing struggle to understand English. "Sonita, Cori would like to tell you something," said Rokhsareh.

I responded with a big smile, signaling my eagerness to hear what Cori had to say. Cori spoke unfamiliar words, and Rokhsareh translated: "Cori has seen and shared your song 'Daughters for Sale' with people and has secured a very good school for you. You have received a full scholarship to go to America to study!" Rokhsareh's excitement was at its peak, and I felt overwhelmed with happiness. "How could this be true?" I wondered aloud, still doubting whether this amazing news was just a dream. Rokhsareh reassured me further, making it easier to believe that I was really going to attend a school on the other side of the world—where they even had music!

I had just received the biggest opportunity of my life, but I was unsure when I could obtain an ID to travel to America. "Where is America?" I asked Rokhsareh. She spread out a map on the ground. "This is Afghanistan," she said, pointing to one area, "and this is America, quite far away."

"Why is it yellow? Is it all desert?" I asked, worried that traveling to the other side of the world might mean not seeing my family for a long time. It was one of many questions I had.

"Can we get an ID here in Iran instead of in Afghanistan?" I asked Rokhsareh.

"No, you have to get it from Afghanistan," Rokhsareh replied. "That means we have to go back to your family."

"But you know they won't let me leave if they see how far America is from Afghanistan."

"I understand, but there's no choice. Your mother needs to be there when you apply for the ID."

I sighed. "My mom and brothers will never let me leave the country alone," I said.

As Rokhsareh had predicted, there were no alternatives; I had to go to Afghanistan to obtain an ID. We chose a date to leave, and in the days leading up to our departure, I planned to spend more time with Latif and Fadia and to find a way to say a final goodbye to the NGO.

"Don't tell Nana about the scholarship," I told Latif.

"When will you be back?" asked Fadia, as she cried silently.

"I don't know, it might take some time."

"No, come back tomorrow!" Fadia was heartbroken to know that her only friend had a long journey ahead. I walked the familiar streets near the NGO, crying over Fadia's innocence and pure love. I entered the NGO quietly, uncertain whether I was putting the place at greater risk by being there. But I needed to hug my friends before leaving.

I walked in and saw Mrs. Poori's familiar, beautiful face. She gave me a warm hug and whispered in my ear how proud and happy she was for me and my future in America. "I never told you this, but one of my dreams for my children was for them to go and study in a different country," Mrs. Poori said, as she began to wipe away her tears. "You've made that dream come true."

I smiled at her and asked her not to cry about something that was out of her control.

"Don't forget to take your Dreams Book with you," said Mrs. Poori, not knowing that it had been the first thing I had packed.

"Soni!!!" Hasin and Sori both ran into Mrs. Poori's office and hugged me so tightly that I couldn't move my arms to hug them back. "Are you really going to America?" Sori asked with excitement.

"Yes, I'm going to Afghanistan with Rokhsareh tomorrow to get the ID I need!" I said.

"So cool! You're going to learn English!" said Hasin. Since Rokhsareh knew English, I had learned a few words from her: "Hi," "Bye," "I am a rapper," and "This is a pen." After the day I learned about my possible life in America, I purchased a children's book that had about two hundred new words in it. Though I didn't understand 99 percent of them, I still tried. I was getting better at recognizing the English alphabet. To show off, I spoke two or three words in broken English, which impressed Hasin and Sori.

Mrs. Poori agreed to let Sori and Hasin miss class so we could talk in the backyard.

"Do you remember when we did that fake interview where you told our imaginary audience to line up for your signature?" Hasin recalled. "Now it sounds like you're really that person." We all laughed. Though we looked happy, deep down, we all struggled to let go of each other.

"I'll visit you, I promise," I said, feeling my true emotions surface. When I left, I gave Sori and Hasin each something to remember me by. They were going to always be in my heart, no matter how far away I was taken by the future I wanted to build.

It took us two days to persuade Iranian police officers that I was actually from Afghanistan. It's ironic: in Iran, I struggled to fit in as an Iranian, and at the border, I struggled to prove that I was an Afghan.

As the car took us farther from Iran, I felt closer to home. The dusty road had been paved, and there were fewer broken houses. I kept my eyes open for several hours, observing the place I had come from. There was so much to see and share with Rokhsareh, who didn't seem to be scared to enter Afghanistan.

Then we arrived at the address I had given the driver. "Is this it?" Rokhsareh asked.

"Maybe, I don't know," I said and knocked on the door.

"Coming!" I heard a soft child's voice—Reza, Razeq's son. He opened the door with Zia and we all began to scream with excitement. "Nana, Sonita is here!" Zia hugged me.

Nana arrived at the door behind Razeq and Zaher. It felt so nice to be home. Everyone seemed so kind and happy that I was tempted several times to tell the truth when they asked the reason for my sudden return. But I said only, "I'm here to get a passport."

"Why do you need a passport?" Nana asked. Once again, I lied, "I'm not going anywhere; I just should have one, and Rokhsareh can help me get it." Rokhsareh supported my statement.

I had missed everyone very much, and knowing of the long journey I planned made me miss them even in their presence. "I saw you on TV, Auntie," Reza said.

"So nice!" I exclaimed. "Did you like the song?"

"Yes, I even remember it!"

"Really? I want to hear it," I said. Then Reza surprised me, taking control of the room with my words.

"Nice job, buddy!" Naser encouraged Reza, and I felt as if his applause was aimed at me.

"Do people know you in Iran?" Zia asked, surprised when I said no. "People request your song on the radio here!" I laughed, happy to hear that.

Nana and my brothers only listened and asked no more.

I craved time with my family, but time was against me. After only two days, I had to leave. "We have to fly to Kabul to get a passport," I told Nana and Razeq, who showed less objection than my other brothers.

"Why do you need the passport so badly?" Nana's old question lingered. I responded with old and new lies that eventually convinced Nana.

"Okay, then we'll expect your return next week?" Nana asked, and I responded positively. I lied again and again to make the escape easier. Only Rokhsareh, Zia, and I knew the truth. I couldn't keep such a wonderful opportunity a secret from Zia. She was so happy and supported my decision, even suggesting different ways for me to convince Nana.

When the time came, I left Nana, my brothers, and the kids without saying a proper goodbye. Only Zia and I exchanged a long hug, as she knew I might not come back home. To avoid suspicion, I couldn't even cry. But I let my emotions show once the taxi drove us far away to the airport. I was upset, but also very happy. It was my first time ever traveling by plane.

"Is it scary?" I asked Rokhsareh, who assured me of its safety.

The plane took off, mostly with men onboard, because women had no privilege to travel. All the men, young and old, spoke of how small Herat looked from up in the sky. They were right. It looked not only small but also brown, as if no trees had ever been planted there. Mountains and muddy buildings were scattered across the ground, with no green to be found. I looked outside the window for a few minutes more, trying to say goodbye to my family in my heart as I fell asleep.

The scariest part of traveling on a plane is landing, especially when it feels like the plane is running off the runway. Still, we arrived in Kabul safely and headed to the hotel.

There were more women on the streets in Kabul than in Herat, and everything seemed a bit cleaner. However, one thing remained the same: the high level of security. At the hotel entrance, two guards with guns checked our bags. They directed us to the reception desk to check in with another guard. Hoisting a gun on his shoulder, he led us to another room, where more armed men stood by the elevator.

The hotel room was beautiful; I never imagined Afghanistan could have such nice places. Rokhsareh and I unpacked, and after a light meal, we took a taxi to the Afghan Embassy. I was shocked when I saw the line—hundreds of people waiting to get passports! Since I didn't have an Afghan National ID to apply for a passport, the process took even longer than expected. We had to make the same trip to the embassy for a week before we were finally given a date for the passport. I could hardly wait to see my ID. I was as excited about getting it as I was about traveling to the United States to be enrolled in school!

A few days before receiving my passport, I was invited to appear on a morning show on Tolo TV. I was super nervous about my first TV appearance. I excitedly told Zia about the opportunity over the phone. When Nana took the phone, she asked, "When are you coming back to Herat?"

"Soon, I hope," I replied, and quickly directed the conversation back to the Tolo TV appearance.

The next morning, I arrived at the TV station, where I saw even more security. When the program began, questions were thrown at me before I could fully respond to the previous one. I could hardly pay attention, knowing that right after the show we were going to the embassy to get my passport. I succeeded in saying what was important before time was up. Then I rushed with Rokhsareh to the embassy. We waited by the door, and then they called my name, "Sonita Alizadeh."

Before handing me the passport, the man at the embassy said, "You look very impatient. What's the rush?"

"I'm going to America!" I responded proudly, glancing at Rokhsareh holding her camera outside the office.

"Well, go and return once you have something to offer your people, especially me!" He laughed and gave me the passport I had been waiting to see and hold for days, weeks, months, and years.

I held the beautiful, small blue book. "This is mine!" I screamed to Rokhsareh. "I have a passport now!" I opened the first page of it, where I saw the most incredible thing: I had a birthday—they had picked November 11, 1996. It was different from what I had in my Dreams Book, but it was very easy to remember! They had also spelled my last name differently, Alizada instead of Alizadeh, but I didn't mind.

I needed my first name, Sonita, and my picture in an ID. There it was: an old dream in real time.

The day I had been impatiently waiting for finally arrived. Feeling wonderful, I stepped inside the plane headed to Dubai. I sat next to Rokhsareh, who seemed happier than me. Then I sent a final message to Zia, letting her know that I would be leaving soon. She returned to me a long message expressing her excitement for me and that I should try to visit the family soon.

"Last night I had a beautiful dream," I responded.

"Tell me about it."

"In my dream, I was walking in a river. The water was so pure that I could see the big and small rocks on the river floor. It felt so wonderful, and you were in my dream!"

When I told my dream to Rokhsareh, she said, "That is a nice dream." Then I asked her more about the school I was going to. Where was it? Did she have pictures?

"Ha-ha, you'll see it the day after tomorrow!"

As the plane took off, my heart trembled. I ordered my eyes to look out the window, trying to memorize the view of home in case I might not be able to return soon. Deep down, I was happy knowing I was going to be able to write music freely and be in a real school.

When we landed in Dubai, I saw freedom for women for the first time. I put my hand on my hijab, wanting to feel the fresh air in my hair. Hijab, for me, had meant being ordered to live by other people's rules. I took it off and swiftly put it at the bottom of my bag, knowing I wouldn't be forced to wear it anymore. The freedom felt nice, and I wished I could share the feeling with Zia.

On the flight to the United States, I binge-watched several films, and after a few hours, I fell asleep. I woke up when the flight attendant announced our arrival at my final destination. Looking out the window, I didn't see many tall buildings like those in the Spider-Man movies. We couldn't possibly be in the United States! "Where are the tall buildings?" I asked Rokhsareh.

"We're in Utah," she explained.

We left the plane and I met the headmaster of my future school, Mr. Joe Loftin, who reminded me of Mrs. Poori—so kind! He was at the airport to welcome me and Rokhsareh and take us to what he called Wasatch Academy. It was a two-hour drive to the school.

When we got to the small town where the school was, Mr. Loftin stopped by the music building first. I jumped around like a little girl as I walked through it, softly touching pianos, cellos, drums, guitars, and many other instruments I couldn't even name. Mr. Loftin laughed and gave us a tour of the whole building, which was empty of people but filled with music. I wanted to live there forever!

Once the tour was done, we drove to where I was going to live—Zoe Dorm. I didn't know the wonderful surprise that awaited me: I met the lady who had initially discovered me, Cori Stern. "Welcome, Sonita!" said Cori with her beautiful smile and gave me a big hug.

She and her friend Zoe, who also believed in my music, were there to welcome me and show me my room. We walked inside the two-story dorm, which was so nice and clean. My shared room was upstairs in the corner, with a view of the front of the entire school. I entered and saw an empty bed, figuring it must be mine. The other bed in the corner was covered with clothes, books, chips, and everything else: my roommate was going to be messy!

Rokhsareh, Zoe, and Cori chatted as I stood in the middle of the room, trying to understand that my new life wasn't a dream—I was actually in the United States and was going to start school in two days.

Once I put all my belongings in the room, Cori and Zoe drove Rokhsareh and me to a big store called Walmart—a common place, they said. But it was so amazing! And the trip became even more amazing when Cori and Zoe told me to pick out anything I needed for my room. To show my gratitude and not misuse their generosity, I chose only some cleaning supplies, bedsheets, and a few essentials.

Before it got too late, I asked Rokhsareh to stay with me while I mustered the courage to call Nana. When I made the call, Zia answered and asked excitedly where I was. "I've arrived in America. Can I speak to Nana?"

"Where are you?" Nana inquired when she picked up the phone. Overwhelmed and unsure of how to break the news myself, I handed the phone to Rokhsareh. "Sonita received a full scholarship from a very prestigious school, so we had no choice but to come to America," Rokhsareh explained. I anxiously tried to guide her on what to say so Nana wouldn't get too upset. But no matter what we said, Nana became furious with both me and Rokhsareh.

"When will you be back?" Nana demanded.

"Maybe in two or three years," I said.

"What?! Your brothers will not let this happen!" That was the last thing Nana said before abruptly hanging up the phone on me. I was left feeling worried, upset, and defenseless. I hoped she might reconsider and did my best to calm down; maybe a good night's sleep would help me face the situation with a clearer mind.

I spent my first night in the United States staring at my roommate's desk crowded with stuff. I saw a picture in a frame and picked it up, looking at it closely. Two other small photos were on the wall, and in all of them, one face appeared—white, with green eyes and beautifully organized teeth. "She must be my roommate," I told myself with a smile on my face. I already liked her just by looking at her; she looked so quiet and kind. I couldn't wait for the night to pass so I could meet her.

In the morning, a loud bang on the door woke me up. Someone put a key in the lock, and before I could fully open my eyes, a loud voice made me jump from bed. "Good morning, Sonita! I'm Sarah, your roommate!" I had been so wrong; she wasn't quiet at all! But she was still beautiful and looked kind.

"Hi Sarah, I am Sonita," I delivered my memorized sentences as she, one by one, put her suitcases inside the room. I had never met or spoken with Sarah before, but she treated me as if she had known me for years. She was so funny and talkative. She spoke and continued speaking while I, having run out of English sentences, only listened.

Once I had access to the internet, I discovered Google Translate. My mind was blown—I had found a way to communicate with Sarah! I asked hundreds of questions, including the meaning of the word "dude," which Sarah kept calling me. She started or ended every sentence with "dude." After hearing it hundreds of times, it stuck with me, and I had to know what it meant. We became very close friends in just an hour.

Sarah took my phone and typed a long sentence in English, indicating her interest in giving me a tour by bike. "Yes, I like it!" I declared. Sarah reminded me of my childhood wish for a bike, along with so many other controversial hopes I had.

As time passed, the entire dorm slowly filled with parents and students. I thought about how wonderful it must feel for the students to have their parents escort them to school, while I had run away from home to be in school. I wondered whether it was crazy to wish that Nana and my brothers would support my education.

Sarah and I put our hats and gloves on and excitedly ran down the stairs. When I opened the door, a fresh cold air touched my face, waking my entire body. I squinted my eyes as they met white, shiny snow covering the grass. I looked around;

the sky was so beautiful, so clean. If Hasin or Sori were with me, they would say this place was *Behesht* (heaven).

I sat on the rear seat of the bicycle while Sarah, with amusing struggles, managed to carry us along the lightly snow-covered sidewalks. The paths led to more dorms, classrooms, the gym, and the cafeteria, where we stopped for lunch.

"Oh my god! This is incredible!" I exclaimed in Farsi as I entered the dining hall and saw all kinds of edible items—literally all kinds! It felt like a miracle that I no longer had to cook for my family or myself. Since I still couldn't order anything in English, I simply pointed at a cheeseburger. With the first bite, I fell in love with cheeseburgers. So delicious!

Since taking food was allowed, I ordered another cheeseburger and took it to my room. Before it was too late, I called Zia. Nana wasn't home.

"How is life there?" Zia asked. "Tell me all about it!" She was shocked by the freedom and safety I had and the things I saw—like seeing two boys kissing each other.

"So, you don't wear a scarf anymore?" she asked.

"I don't, but for Nana I will wear it when I take pictures or when Nana wants to do a video call."

"She seems so upset with you, so don't expect a call from her anytime soon," said Zia.

"I feel like everyone is mad at me besides you," I said sadly, worried that I would lose my family because of this decision I had made.

"Hurry up, time to leave!" The dorm parents knocked on every door to make sure we were all prepared to be on time for the first day of class. Before I set out, I saw Rokhsareh, who was ready to pack up her belongings and leave. I felt a deep sadness, knowing that although my time for education and music had arrived, my time with Rokhsareh was coming to an end. We shared a long, tight hug before she left to complete her documentary, *Sonita*.

I walked with Sarah until she found her class, and then we parted ways. I wandered around and checked my busy school schedule: 8:00–9:30 ESL, 9:30–11:30 ESL, 12:30–2:00 Lunch, 2:30–4:00 ESL. I wondered what "ESL" meant.

With some help, I found the class. When I opened the door, I saw that most of the students were from China. No one was American. Feeling shy and aware of the language barrier, I chose a seat away from the others.

The room was bigger than I had expected, with a big whiteboard attached to the wall and two big windows and fresh plants all over. On the walls were all kinds of drawings that were fun to look at. Some of the students seemed to be lonely, like me, while some had already made friends and enjoyed speaking in their native languages. The teacher arrived soon after, carrying papers in his hand.

"Hello, teacher," I said and stood up in respect, as we all did in Iran. The teacher, a man in his forties with a bald head and thick glasses, greeted everyone. "I am Mr. John. Welcome to your English as a second language class." Mr. John spoke for about thirty minutes and concluded with a lengthy statement that some of us understood and followed. One by one, the students stood up, introduced themselves, mentioned their country of origin, and stated their grade.

When it was my turn I said, "My name is Sonita Alizada, and I am from Afghanistan." I didn't mention my grade, since I didn't know—and didn't mind, as long as I could stay in school and move on to the next grade when I was ready. The first day of classes passed without me learning much of anything; I understood only about 5 percent of whatever was said. At the end of the day, I received a substantial amount of homework.

During the first week of school, I often locked myself in my room, crying until I felt less homesick. In Iran, I had never felt this way because I had Sori, Hasin, and Nazif. Now I was so far from home that when I was awake, they were asleep.

A few days later, I took a bus to Walmart, where I witnessed something shocking. While waiting in line to check out, I saw a man with two young women and about five kids. I wondered about his relationship with the women, and a friend later told me that some Mormons practice polygamy. I was devastated to think that the two young women I saw might have been forced into marriage, like Sori, Hasin, and Nazif, and even myself.

As time passed, I began to understand English a little more. The day I received a laptop, I started my mission to learn whether child marriage happened in the United States, the country they called "the land of the free." I found sources, including the website of Girls Not Brides, a global organization working to end child marriage, which stated that every year, about fifteen million girls around the world are forced into marriage before the age of eighteen. I couldn't believe it. I watched YouTube videos of child marriage surveyors in Florida. Angry, I kept asking myself if there was any place on the earth where such a practice is banned.

As I grappled with this reality, I received the greatest news from Rokhsareh: an Iranian woman had arranged for my first concert in California, where Sarah was from. A week before the concert, I turned my room into a stage and practiced the songs I was going to perform, including my first, "Daughters for Sale."

The day arrived, and I was invited to stand on a real stage with about three hundred people in front of me. My God, it felt amazing and thrilling to see my greatest dream come true! As I rapped, I looked at the faces in the audience and everyone looked invested. After a few songs, my heart began to beat again at its normal pace. *What a wonderful feeling to be alive*, I thought.

After the concert, I saw a line of people waiting to take my picture or just to simply encourage me to continue rapping. I sent pictures to Sori and Zia. I couldn't wait for them to see that I had met my greatest dream and to understand that they should hold tight to theirs.

19

Sonita

I hadn't yet regained the energy I spent to escape my fate when I decided that I wanted to be more than just a rapper and a student. I wanted—I *needed*—to be an activist. A *raptivist*, as others called it.

In 2016, Rokhsareh's documentary *Sonita*, which took three years to make, was finally ready to be released. It was time to share my story—and the story of millions of other girls around the world. I wasn't happy about being so public. I wasn't worried about being recognized, in fact, I liked it! But I often felt shy to speak—especially when my audience was made up of English speakers. My heart pounded whenever I had to speak in front of people. But I felt it would be wrong to have all these privileges while my friends and other girls continued to be tortured by a practice I was once a victim of—and was now its biggest enemy. I had to speak up.

The first screening of the movie was in Norway. I arrived at a big theater where about five hundred people had gathered to watch. It was sold out. I sat next to Rokhsareh, who was the only person who knew that the girl whom five hundred people were seated to watch was there among the audience. I felt nervous because I hadn't seen the film and wasn't sure what to expect.

The film began with me cutting images out of magazines and pasting them in my Dreams Book. I smiled and felt excited to see what came next. Sometimes I was drawn in by one particular memory brought on by the images in the film, and the laughter of the audience would bring me back to the present. I could feel their heartbreak when Nana tried to sell me into marriage, but for me, it was normal.

What really broke my heart was the scene that I love and hate the most, which brings me to tears each time I watch the film: Fadia begging me to return to Iran the next day. It made me think about how much I missed her, my family, my friends, and the places I knew. It upset me to see my niece desperately pleading with her only friend not to leave her, and know that I did anyway. I wondered whether the kids in her neighborhood still refused to play with her. Fadia reminded me of everything I had when I was her age, including Ranjita. Her innocent eyes in the film looked just like Ranjita's.

I felt so strange sitting in the middle of hundreds of people, watching the struggle I had gone through and still couldn't let go of, even years later. I hurried to distract myself with the positive moments shown in the film so I could prepare for my surprise performance. Before the film ended, Rokhsareh handed me the mic, signaling that it was time for my rap song "Daughters for Sale."

As the film credits rolled and the background music played, I began to rap from among the audience. People were stunned; the couple sitting next to me looked amazed that the person whose three-year story they had followed for the previous ninety minutes was seated right next to them. As I walked toward the stage, people stood up in respect, smiling warmly at me.

That performance felt so wonderful, but by the end, the questions I received from the audience broke my heart. The takeaway from the film seemed to be that my mother was a monster. One person asked, “Do you even love her?”—not understanding that Nana had tried to do what she believed was best for me.

After a tour in Europe, I attended the Sundance Film Festival, where the film was shown. There I was confronted with questions like, “What is child marriage?” “Is your story real?” “Does it snow in Afghanistan?” These questions revealed to me that many people in Europe and America were as unaware of the world beyond their own as I had been. Despite having the world at their fingertips with internet access, they didn’t seem to know much about many of the issues I thought were common knowledge. They were unfamiliar with the struggles I shared, just as I was unfamiliar with their lifestyle—filled with nightlife, sports games, and other activities.

I was disheartened that some people, even those who have access to the internet and a top-notch education, remain unaware of what life is like beyond their own country. Many students I encountered complained about having to go to school, while for millions of other kids around the world, that opportunity is a distant dream. It pained me to hear some of these students speak ungratefully about their parents, who probably had worked long hours to provide them with an education. These kids seemed unaware of the immense privilege they had, taking it for granted rather than appreciating it and knowing what a dream they were living.

The lack of awareness on the issue close to my heart made me push myself harder. I memorized my story in English so I could begin raising awareness in high schools through the film and my music. As emotionally challenging as it was to relive my story, it did make my experiences more real for those I encountered.

Performing "Daughters for Sale" took me back to the days when I was about to be sold into marriage, the day I saw Nazif with bruises on her face, and the time that Sori tried to commit suicide. Despite the pain, I wanted people to know that this story is not over and that they should take action in any way they can.

With the help of Zoe and Cori, my activism was featured on news channels such as CNN, BBC, ABC, Voice of America, and many more. As someone who had never had the chance to speak before, it was overwhelming to see the world now wanting to listen.

Eventually, without my realizing it, my speeches reached Afghanistan. When Zia told me, "Nana paid a translator to translate your talks into Farsi," I knew I was making a difference, starting with my family.

One day, before a math test—my weakest subject—I received a call from Nana. I left the class to take the call, as Nana usually avoided speaking with me. We talked, and she sounded so sweet and caring. "Be sure not to eat pork or drink wine," Nana said, reminding me of a few things every Muslim must avoid. I didn't mention to her that I was slowly losing interest in religion.

I was so sad when I heard that my uncle had cut ties with Nana for letting me stay in an infidel country. She was enduring so much pressure from society, yet her soft words showed only how much she missed me. As always, I was waiting for that wonderful and final approval of my work and self. I had heard "I am proud of you" from thousands of strangers in America, but I needed only one person to say it: Nana.

"Also, I want you to make a song about Farkhondeh," said Nana, mentioning a woman who had been killed by angry men in Kabul for being falsely accused of disrespecting Islam.

Before hanging up, I asked Nana if my brothers were okay. Her hesitation showed that they were still struggling to come to terms with my new life in America. "They looked less angry when they saw you on BBC still wearing a hijab," Nana said.

Before hanging up, Zia shared with me something life-changing that proved to me I had already made a difference. "You know, the other day a suitor came asking for my hand, and Nana actually asked me if I wanted to marry or not. Isn't that crazy?" said Zia quietly, as if she were afraid to speak of Nana's sudden beautiful change.

"This is what I wanted to hear! Tell me more!" I said to Zia. The change in Nana's behavior was so overwhelming that I messed up my math test. But it was worth it to stand in the hall, talking with Zia about a dream coming true.

Knowing that I'd made a difference at home, I pushed myself even harder. When my long break from school arrived, with the help of Wasatch Academy and the Strongheart Group I began to travel more to share my story with the little broken English I knew. I returned to school when time required me to change my role from being an activist to being a student, but I remained both at the same time.

As school began again, I promised myself not to let my activism exhaust me and distract me from my schoolwork. I missed my friend Sarah, who graduated from the academy, but at a parent-student lunch I attended, I met a girl named Christina, who had a beautiful smile and green eyes, and another girl named Morsal, with curly hair and a muscular build. Christina was from Colorado, and her father had escorted her to her first day of school. But I wasn't the only student without parents or friends there; Morsal seemed to be in a similar situation.

Once everyone was seated, my greatest fear arrived: ordering food in front of English speakers. I was shy to speak and didn't know the menu except for a picture of fried potatoes. Christina understood my struggle and asked me something in English. Since my response wasn't very understandable, it proved to her that I needed extra help. So, she took out the mighty Google Translate and helped me order food.

Over the course of the year, I met Christina's family, and even became a part of it. For the first time in my life, I experienced Christmas. I received so many gifts—something I had never experienced before. Since that day, Christmas became my favorite holiday, and gradually, I started to forget my childhood's most loved holiday, Eid. It wasn't hard to forget; Eid without family and friends didn't mean much to me.

Christina's family was so open-minded and fun. I'll never forget the day I made them laugh when I accidentally ate pork and exclaimed, "I love it!" I also tried wine, but didn't enjoy it, so I stuck to eating pork. I understood why it might be forbidden in Islam. It was so delicious! And in my experience, Islam forbade whatever was good and fun.

When Christina and I returned to school after staying at her family's house for a break, I discovered that my new roommate was Mari, the most notorious troublemaker at the school. "Yo, bitch," she greeted me. She was a lesbian, tall with short hair, fair skin, and long earrings. I liked her, but she was a lot messier than Sarah had been. She loved smoking weed and had a pile of clothing, both dirty and clean, mixed together. She also had two different backpacks: one was filled with school supplies, and the other contained sex toys. Often, she would hide the sex toys under my bed, knowing that the dorm parent had no reason to check my side.

Whenever she got high, she would shout from her group circle, "Sonita and I have kissed!" Everyone would laugh. I didn't mind the joking; everyone in the dorm knew I wasn't attracted to girls. But Morsal, whose room was next to mine, doubted that.

One day at lunch, Morsal joined Christina and me at our table. She asked if I could teach her how to play chess after school, and I agreed. After school and dinner, I went to her room to start the lesson. She was alone when I arrived.

"I watched your movie on Netflix," she said with a smile. "You're famous!"

"Ha-ha, famous to you, maybe," I replied. She looked at me in a way that was different from other girls. It felt strange. Throughout the chess lesson, she seemed distracted. As I was about to leave, she asked, "Can I have a hug?" I gave her a hug and got lost in her warm embrace. I felt small standing next to her, with my head near her chest. She smelled so fresh and pleasant that I didn't mind her long, tight hug.

She sent a Snapchat later: "Can we play tomorrow too?" I said yes.

My group of friends began to tease me. "She likes you, Sonita," they would say. I would laugh, knowing that in my culture, liking someone of the same sex meant a simple friendship. Outside of friendship, there was no way a girl could love another girl romantically. "You might be gay, actually, since you rejected that guy for prom," said my friend Christina, not knowing that I didn't find US boys to be attractive. Most of them seemed interested in video games and had a certain softness that didn't appeal to me.

"Please," I told my friends, "I would puke if I kissed a girl." That ended all their doubts.

On Valentine's Day, I received a beautiful gift from Morsal: a delicate ring and a long letter expressing how grateful she was to have met me. There was so much love in her letter, but she didn't confess any romantic feelings for me. All my friends laughed and rolled on the ground as I read it.

Another long break arrived, and I left school with Christina. Morsal sent me text messages whenever she had a break from basketball practices. "Can I request you as my new roommate?" she asked over text while she was in Portugal, preparing to return to the United States. I was confused; I knew I didn't have romantic feelings for her, but I also knew that when she didn't reach out, I felt disappointed.

I shared the news in my group chat with my three friends from Kenya and Christina. "Oh my god, finally you'll get some privacy to kiss each other, ha-ha," Purity said, and the others added to the teasing.

When I arrived at school, I felt so nervous about seeing Morsal and hated my strange behavior. I opened the door and awkwardly gave her a hug. "I missed you, stupid," she said and gave me a second hug.

Morsal joined us for dinner, and my friends, who were already fond of her, were thrilled to have her with us. We all played basketball, dividing into two teams: the five friends versus just Morsal on her own. Despite five against one, Morsal managed to score more points than all of us; after all, she was the best female basketball player at school. I returned early to my room to do some homework before the start of the semester, which looked difficult with calculus, geography, chemistry, and biology classes.

Morsal came back from the game, and we talked about our classes and our favorite teacher before getting ready for bed. I turned off the lights and said goodnight. "Really? Without a hug?" asked Morsal, seated on her bed with her legs hanging off the edge.

I stood by my bed, looking at her face illuminated by the light streaming in from our two large windows. I walked over to her bed. She opened her arms, and I wrapped my arms around her neck as she began to breathe near my ear. I was about to let go, but she held me even tighter. She quickly put me on her bed and held herself over me. We looked at each other, breathing heavily and erratically. With her hand locked in mine, I felt under her control. I could move or say no, but I didn't. Something so unique was awakening within me that I never had been aware of.

I no longer felt any shame or hesitation about intimacy. As I was lost in the intoxicating mix of sensations, she pressed her lips against mine. We kissed, and I loved it! I loved my new sin; I wanted to be drowned in it and commit it again.

It was such a beautiful night. The moon outside became our candle, and the crickets played us a melody that perfectly harmonized with the sound of our kisses and small movements on the tiny bed. I felt transformed into a different person—one who cared less about customs and limitations. As a child and a youth, I was always told that the most valuable thing I had was my virginity. I gave it to Morsal with pleasure.

Just at the beginning of a new semester, I was already distracted. Sitting in math class, as Mrs. Marga, our teacher, explained the lesson, I repeated the story of the night before in my head, over and over. With each recall, I felt a deeper desire for Morsal. She felt the same way about me.

When I shared what had happened over lunch with Christina, Purity, Sheila, and Ashley, they all began to laugh. "Oh my god, did I tell you that you look and act gay?" Christina said, laughing along with the rest. I looked at them, trying to calm them down as everyone was staring at our table.

"Guys, please shut the fuck up," I said. "Forget about it."

How could I tell Nana that I was no longer a virgin? That was way worse than eating pork, drinking wine, and taking off my hijab. Still, Morsal was worth more than any guy I might have given my virginity to. She cared so much for me that every day she wrote a short love note and left it on my desk. Each time I had a performance, she was there to support me, and each time she had a basketball game, I was there to cheer her on. We kept our relationship a secret from most people, but my friends and Zia knew.

"What does that mean, that you are in love with a girl? Like friendship?" Zia asked over the phone when I shared my love story with her.

"No, I mean I love, love her," I replied.

"So, she is your best, best friend?"

"NO, I mean I have romantic feelings for her."

"*Astaghfirullah*!" Zia exclaimed. "What are you saying, Sister?"

"I kissed her, and I like her like a guy."

"Eww! So disgusting even to imagine," Zia said. "You are really lost, Sister!"

Like Zia, I also struggled to understand the new me, but I liked who I was. I enjoyed my relationship with Morsal until our graduation arrived, and then we had to go our separate ways. It was hard, unbearable even, but it didn't mean that we would never see each other again.

I was sad but also very happy to be the first generation in my family to graduate from high school, but at the same time, I was sad to leave Morsal to go to Bard College, after being rejected from multiple colleges because of my low English test scores.

Morsal and I had a long goodbye, assuring each other that we would stay in each other's hearts no matter how far we went. As we separated, I felt great pain, but at the same time, I was proud of myself for giving myself the chance to love her.

20

The Fall of Afghanistan

I took a gap year after high school to address my homesickness and my desire to fully reengage with my activism. I spent a year in Washington, DC, studying English and using my story and music to raise awareness about child marriage. Since I finally could understand and speak English better, I was invited to high-profile events, not only to perform but also to share my experience.

Sometimes my presentation would follow so-called world leaders talking about big issues even though some of them had zero understanding of them. They talked about women's rights in the Middle East while women in the United States faced injustice. They spoke about safety, when all their carelessness added to tensions in Third World countries. They discussed ending poverty while thousands of dollars were spent on gatherings like ours, where people like us showed up and delivered speeches. At each event I attended, I saw massive venues with fancy lunch menus and bags of goodies. The money wasted on these gatherings could feed thousands of people in a poor country.

I had thought that being at all these "important" events

could make a change, but I learned I was just there to entertain them with my music and unbearable story. I wondered about the people who kept eating while I told them about girls being sexually harmed through forced marriages.

I knew that an issue as big as child marriage couldn't be solved in such a short time and by a small group of people, but I saw that not much attention was paid to it, even after I shared my story. Over time, I became increasingly aware of the idea that some human rights issues had to remain issues, so the profitable business of human rights would continue to benefit some people.

The United Nations established seventeen Sustainable Development Goals (SDGs), with child marriage being a part of Goal 5, which focuses on achieving gender equality. I was unhappy that child marriage wasn't given its own distinct goal, despite the fact that it involves issues as serious as rape. How disappointing! The countries that had produced the Universal Declaration of Human Rights in 1948 appeared to treat those rights as though they were worth less than the paper on which they were printed.

I was mentally exhausted, but I didn't stop. I spoke even louder, urging NGOs to take a different direction to better solve the issue. Most of the time, their response was to give me awards and invite me to share my story again. I became frustrated, but I continued to work with them, hoping they might eventually take meaningful action.

When I was invited to share my story at the United Nations again, I noticed that none of the portraits on the wall of UN leaders were of women. Yet, I was there to talk about women and equality. I found myself questioning the hypocrisy of some of the credible NGOs around the world and the tendency of people to overlook and not challenge the injustices present within these so-called human rights defenders.

The lack of meaningful action from NGOs began to make me feel indifferent about running around and sharing my story, hoping it would awaken the sleeping leaders. I was so young and inexperienced, and I kept putting aside my life to tell my tale again and again until everything exhausted me. I got to the point where I could no longer pay attention to anyone.

At one event hosted by Microsoft cofounder Bill Gates, I sat in a chair listening to President Barack Obama speak about important subjects that I cannot recall. As he spoke, I tried to focus on his words, but my tired brain kept distracting me with thoughts like, *Oh, his shoelaces are tied so neatly, oh, look, his tie is nice. Wow, that guy behind him has a big nose.* My mind was filled with questions and irrelevant thoughts. And yet people still invited me to do more. I felt so much pressure to continue, having been named the voice of women facing child marriage.

My biggest mistake as an activist was that I thought I had to run around and share my story even when it was hurting me. I forgot that in order to perform better, I had to understand that I wasn't just what people saw—a strong girl. I should have remembered that, like many other people, I was a simple girl who needed to do normal activities too.

The voice people put in my head was that I was a force of nature with endless energy. In truth, I was tired; so many times, I felt weak and just wanted to sleep; talk to my family, to Fadia, to Sori and Hasin, and friends; watch a scary movie; and do my nails with other girls.

I had learned this after four years of intense activism. So I took it easy in 2019, when I arrived at Bard College in upstate New York. Just before my arrival, snow had covered the whole campus, making it difficult to get around and meet people, but I still managed to make up for all the time in my life that passed without having lasting fun.

Enjoying life at a college with about three thousand students came naturally. During the first week, only the five hundred incoming freshmen were on campus. I pushed through, despite having a roommate who, unlike Sarah, wasn't a fan of talking. But soon the rest of the students returned, and I met Emily and Khadija, another Afghan girl I loved spending time with.

After two weeks, classes started. I was impatient to attend my music and human rights classes, as I had a strong interest in both subjects. My classes were spread out across the campus, which felt great, walking from one class to the next. Because of Bard's natural beauty, I fell in love with nature, forgetting that the big city I had seen in films, New York City, was just two hours away. I bonded with the green campus, the trees, the river, and the birds that woke me up with their singing every single day.

As a student, I could continue my advocacy work through music and social media, while also working part-time—as a photographer, farmer, tour guide, and driver—to support my family back in Afghanistan and to help Khaleq attend barber school. Zia told me, "He often wants to thank you for sending us money, but he's not used to it." Khaleq used to argue with me about quitting school and getting married, but once I was able to financially support the family in a way that none of my brothers had been able to do, they became more understanding and no longer pressured me to return and get married.

Knowing that my family was once again in my life and loved me, I was able to enjoy life at a level I had never before experienced.

One weekend, I went out with some friends to a party on the other side of campus. Until then, I had tried only a sip of wine, but that night, I got drunk for the first time. Initially, I cried a lot, overwhelmed by flashbacks from my childhood. But once I started to feel lighter, I began dancing and singing like never before. My friends were surprised to see new aspects of my personality coming to the surface with the force of alcohol.

That night, I began to understand why many American kids often say, "Yeah, let's go party!" Partying was fun—something that I had never had the opportunity to experience before.

Seven years had passed, and I hadn't seen my family. WhatsApp became the way we stayed connected. Through daily video calls, I watched Nana age and saw Zia become a professional painter, Khaleq open a barber shop, and Razeq's kids grow up. And it brought me great joy to see Fadia and Latif separated from Jabbar, living a nice life with Razeq in Iran where Sori, who was now single and finishing her education, usually visited them. I longed to see my family in person, even for just five minutes, but it was impossible. The level of discrimination against Muslims in the United States meant there was no guarantee I could return home if I had visited them.

"I want to come see you guys," I told Nana during a video call.

"You must be out of your mind," she said. "Now is the most

dangerous time to return, especially after your song against the president, Ashraf Ghani."

She didn't know that every time I heard about a suicide bombing in Herat, I felt as if I had died and come back to life only after learning that my family was safe. I often had nightmares about my relatives harming my immediate family or the Taliban shooting at me or my family members. Whenever I felt homesick, I ran to my favorite spot, Blithewood at Bard, an old mansion with gardens, where it was easier to write music and cry. At night, the sky looked like the nights in Herat, where the stars gathered to light up the sky. The sounds of birds, the rustling leaves, and the river reminded me that life must go on.

When the COVID-19 pandemic hit, I was among the students who had nowhere to go. I stayed on a campus that, once filled with happy faces and music, had turned as quiet as a ghost town. But quarantine hit me the hardest on August 15, 2021, when the Taliban overthrew the Afghan government.

The night before, I had barely slept, as my concerns for my family and country piled up. I sat on my bed watching Instagram live videos showing the Taliban pouring into Herat. How could this be real? My childhood monsters were once again in my hometown, running and hurting, shooting anyone who objected to their arrival.

How broken I felt, crying as I watched the Taliban take over my beloved country—the one to which I had planned to return right after graduation. Latif's words, "I heard gunshots in the background when I called Zia," filled me with dread. In my panic, I left my quarantine room and wandered around aimlessly, trying to breathe while repeatedly calling Zia, but there was no response.

I returned to my room, wondering whether the feelings I had were worse than the people in Afghanistan witnessing the Taliban takeover, as I could do nothing but feel utterly useless and paralyzed.

With no roommate and half of the dorm to myself, I took the opportunity to let out my sadness. I cried out loud and called whoever came to mind who could check on my family. That day, I had class, but I was feeling so down that I turned off my Zoom camera, continuing my sad search for my family. Once it became clear that my country would once again be the shelter for the Taliban, I gave up on the news and continued to make calls. Hours later, I finally got a message from Zia saying, "We are fine. We left home and sheltered in our relative Habib's basement." I cried with relief.

My whole body began to shiver after I learned that they were safe. My bed, which used to be the sweetest spot, now felt like a prison. I was haunted by images of injured people bleeding and the Taliban with their guns running through my childhood's sacred town.

I remember that in my international relations class, I was told I could be a good leader for my country. Now, I felt like I was a woman without a country, stateless after the Taliban announced their victory, handed to them by the United States and the cowardly Afghan president, Ashraf Ghani.

I sat up and tried to eat ramen noodles; it was all that I had to eat. I remembered a movie I had seen a while earlier, *The Terminal*. In the movie, the character played by Tom Hanks was stuck in an airplane terminal after war broke out in his country. He was told he was no longer a citizen of anywhere. I felt his pain deeply after seeing on social media that the Afghan flag—green, red, and black—had been replaced by the black and white Taliban flag. Where was my home now? For how long would I be deprived of my country again?

I began to hate all the Muslim states for backing away from the murder and rape of women carried out in the name of Islam, while none of them stood against the atrocities of the Taliban. I had learned in my international relations class that all countries were selfish and cruel to one another if it benefited them. The world had let down the Afghan women fighting for their rights—the little freedom they gained after twenty years of hard and risky work.

The United Nations did act, but only through a simple tweet. How disappointing! While the Taliban forced women into marriage with their soldiers, pushed them away from public life, and closed school doors to girls above the sixth grade, the international community, the NGOs, the activists all did the same thing: they used social media to condemn the Taliban, as if the Taliban cared about what they tweeted. Anyone could do such a small act against the enormous pushback of Afghan women!

That night I finally got a call from Zia. It was nice to hear that everyone was safe. "Where were you when the city got messy?" I asked Zia.

"We were at home but left to go to Shadijan village once the gunshots increased," she said.

"Is everyone okay?"

"The kids are still afraid, but here we don't hear or see people screaming and running around," she said.

"How long can you stay there?"

"We don't know. There's no way we can go back home because our neighbor saw a group of Talibs around their house trying to get in."

I was so concerned by this last sentence that, right after the call, I decided to reach out to anyone I knew to help my family get out of Afghanistan. It was a painful night. While everyone and everything slept, the wind quietly played with the leaves, and the moon slowly left room for the sun, but I was still awake, going through all my emails, trying to see who else I could reach. I emailed all the people and NGOs to whom I had given my time and energy free of cost. But all I received back from them was, "Sorry, we can't do anything."

But I didn't give up. I couldn't. I reached out to people I found through internet searches, trying to rent a charter plane to evacuate people at risk. No matter how much paperwork I did every day instead of schoolwork, I still did not receive any hopeful response.

After a few days, I sent a little bit more money to my relatives to purchase whatever my family needed to survive.

During this terrible time, Bard was so supportive. The faculty members saw my struggle, and they let me take it a little easy and return my delayed homework after filing my family's case. I thought attending class in person could help my emotional state, so I headed to class.

My photography and human rights professor, Gilles Peress, knew how I felt. He tried not to ask a lot about my country, knowing that I wasn't in a good place to talk about losing my home.

While I was in class, I received another email from an NGO letting me know there was nothing they could do. Reading the email, I wanted to give up. Gilles was a strict teacher who wanted students to be present and active. I was sorry to be there with such bad energy. I was about to ask him if I could leave when he gave the whole class work to do. He came and sat next to me.

"Is your family okay?" he asked.

"I don't really know," I said. "They say they are okay for now."

"I have a friend, Elizabeth Rubin, who's a journalist. You should get in touch with her because she might be able to help," he said. The moment Gilles gave me Elizabeth's number, I left the class to call her. She was busy but soon returned my call. Unlike the hundreds of other people who had heard about my family's situation, she didn't require much when I told her what I was looking for. She asked me for some information and IDs.

Elizabeth was a *New York Times* reporter who had traveled to Afghanistan a few times and was committed to helping people. She was working on raising funds to rent a charter plane, which would depart from Mazar in the northwest of Afghanistan. The next day, I was so relieved when I got a text from her asking me to relocate my family to Mazar. Right after our call, I booked flights for my family, getting them to Mazar the same day.

Once there, Khaleq told me, "Life seems to be a little more peaceful here." He was relieved to be away from Herat, where some people had known about my family's connection to me. Elizabeth helped my family stay in a wedding hall, where about two hundred people were hidden because of their work with the former government.

Two weeks passed, and the plane that was supposed to arrive never did. My family and the others waiting for it didn't dare to see the sun; they stayed inside until the day the chartered plane finally arrived.

I woke up in the morning with a text from Zia: "They said the plane is here. Now we are going to the airport!" I felt a mix of excitement and fear. The airport there was counted to be risky after experiencing multiple explosions. I waited and paced inside my room.

I don't recall how many hours passed—it was so long before I received a picture and a message saying that my family was in Macedonia. Finally, I felt alive again. To celebrate and treat myself, I took a day off and avoided social media.

But I was back on it before too long. This situation, where women, half the population, were confined to their homes, broke my heart. I couldn't do much but constantly use social media to speak out and share stories.

That night, my family video-called, with big smiles on their faces. I felt relieved to learn that they were at a hotel where they could finally get some rest and release their minds from the fear of being taken by the Taliban. After a few weeks, Zia and Yalda, Razeq's daughter, slowly began to feel the freedom I had once discovered—freedom to not wear a hijab. "I love it here, so much! We can even play soccer!" said Zia. The kids got used to the new lifestyle quickly.

But Nana still wore her long hijab. "I left home—this is the only thing that reminds me where I come from," said Nana when we tried to get her to feel the freedom to choose. She was happy the way she was, and we were happy with her decision.

Calling family every day made me feel both sad and good: we had no one left in Afghanistan.

21

Together Again

My family stayed in a safe hotel in Macedonia for nine months. The Open Society Foundations covered all the costs for them, and other Afghan families, until they were accepted to their final destination, Canada. When I called them, they gave me the news. They were in their hotel room with loud music and other women celebrating the journey ahead. “You have to learn English, Nana,” I said, and she responded with a cheerful, “Yes, yes,” making everyone in the room laugh at her newfound goofiness.

In Macedonia, Nana didn’t have to worry about what to eat the next day or, more crucially, whether we would survive another day. Even with these worries behind her, she still seemed sad sometimes, sitting alone and watching news about Afghanistan. It already felt like a distant memory, and it became even more unreachable once they landed in Canada, in June 2022.

It had been about eight years since I had last seen my family; I was overwhelmed with excitement when they called to let me know they were only about an eight-hour drive away from me. I reached out to some American friends, asking them for a sweet spot on the American and Canadian border where I could see my family. Most people advised me to wait until my green card was approved so I could legally cross the border. However, I knew that it would be months before either I or my family would have an ID that would allow us to meet in person.

I stopped taking my friends' advice, opened my laptop, and checked all the potential locations for a reunion. Every place I looked at had a massive body of water between the two countries. I was unsure of whether we would successfully spot each other at Niagara Falls, our determined meeting point. I instructed everyone to wear a specific color so I could easily see them from the American side of the falls.

Early in the morning, I picked up my friend Norin and we drove to Niagara Falls. My family called constantly—"How far away are you?"—making me even more impatient. I shared my excitement out loud with my friend—interrupting every song we listened to in the car; I think I drove him crazy until we arrived, after eight hours of driving.

"Oh my god, this is so crazy, I need to breathe!" I told Norin as I searched for the red T-shirt I had brought to wear so my family could spot the color. We parked the car and looked around. "Where are you guys?" I asked Zia.

"We're near a big tent, and all wearing red."

The moment I arrived near the edge of the falls, I saw something so funny: most of the people on the Canadian side were wearing red. "Ha-ha, I'm so stupid!" I laughed with Norin because I hadn't realized that red was associated with the Canadian flag. Most of the people on the other side looked red. "Good luck!" Norin jokingly said, as I made another call to find my family.

Sadly, the cliffs were located far away from each other, making it impossible for me to see any familiar faces without using binoculars. So I ran to the car, grabbed all the quarters I had, and put them into the binoculars. I put my eye to them and moved around to see. “I can’t see you, wave for me,” I told Zia on the phone while I was trying to find them.

Then, “Oh my god, I see you! I see them!” I said aloud, making Norin laugh and film my crazy binocular family reunion.

“We see you too!” said Zia, using her friend’s fancy camera to zoom in. I don’t know how much I spent on the binoculars that day, but I only stopped looking at my family when I ran out of minutes and quarters.

Seeing them with binoculars kind of felt like using WhatsApp, but this was so much better. The feeling, the timing, and the energy were so real that I felt like I was with them on the other side, giving them a big hug. How I wished I could cross the bridge between Canada and the United States, or even just stand halfway to see my family, to see how happy Nana looked, how refreshed Zia felt, how much fun Razeq’s kids were having playing around, and how glad Khaleq was to see me.

“What if I tried to cross that bridge?” I asked Norin, who had been seated on the grass for half the day.

“Probably they’ll shoot you without giving you a chance to see your family—ha-ha,” he replied. I already knew the problems involved, but I still asked.

We all stayed at the same location for a few hours and only left once Zia’s friend, who was their guide, had to leave. I said goodbye to them as Yalda and Zia cried on the phone. I too felt like crying, frustrated that my family was so close, and yet so far. "I'll come see you soon. And that time we will hug, I promise," I said, and wished them a safe trip back.

Norin and I stayed, went on the boat trip, got refreshed by the wet wind, and started back in the car once we ran out of energy. We slept in the car that night and were on our way to Bard early in the morning.

Once I knew my family was safe, I again received straight As in my classes. I was also inspired to continue engaging in more activism. In addition to passing my final senior exams with the support of Bard faculty members, I succeeded in winning a Global Rhodes Scholarship. This opportunity would allow me to pursue my master's degree in music and politics at the University of Oxford.

I did everything in my power to have my family there for my college graduation, but sadly, it wasn't possible. I was still happy on that day because my American family and friends were in the audience, cheering for me as I received my college degree. It was definitely one of the greatest nights of my life.

Once I got back to my room and sat down, I received a video from Zia of Nana. She was seated on the floor, waiting for me to appear on the live graduation program. When she heard my name, she began to clap for me. Even though Nana wasn't physically with me, she had been seated for six hours until my turn arrived and I received my diploma.

"Is she proud?" I asked Zia, hoping to hear the simple sentence I always wished to hear from Nana.

"Of course she is," Zia replied in the text message.

That day, I partied and danced so much! It was an amazing time in my life that I will always remember.

Just after my graduation, I applied for a Canadian visa and was devastated when it was denied. I no longer could stay at Bard, either, so I was lucky that my friend Laurie offered for me to stay at her beautiful place in New York City. It was an opportunity to finally experience the city I had always wished to see. Living there was an unbelievable experience.

Finally, in August 2023—six months after graduation—I received my green card. I felt wonderful, and free, holding it in my hands. I kept texting and calling everyone I knew to share the news that I was finally going to see my family. The next day, Christina's mom, my American mother, arrived. In the morning, I loaded her car with everything that had belonged to me during the years I was away, and hit the long road to Canada.

Even with a green card, I was still so nervous when the border patrol officer asked me, "Where are you going?" I told him. Before I blurted out that I was truly dying for this moment to arrive, he gave my green card back and told us to go ahead. Wow! I felt unreal, unbearably happy, when I saw a sign that said "Welcome to Canada."

It was going to happen—I was finally going to see my family! Nothing could stop it, I kept telling myself as the car sped along. As the sun set, we passed valleys, several highways, and big towns. The remaining time ticked down on the GPS—three hours, two hours, one hour—and then the voice of the GPS announced, "You have reached your destination."

We pulled up near a five-story building surrounded by small shops. "You made it, girlfriend!" said Cathrine, my American mother, who was so kind to have made this trip with me before she returned to her family in Colorado.

I had made it! I walked up to the building feeling unexpectedly shy. I wondered where this strange, new feeling was coming from—shy around my own family? How odd. I texted Zia, "I'm here!"

It took my family a little while to respond, as if they needed a moment to prepare for my arrival. Finally, I heard footsteps approaching from behind the closed door. When it opened, the first person I saw was Nana. I hugged her tightly, tears streaming down my face, as I breathed in the familiar scent from my childhood that I had longed for.

Then I hugged Zia, my childhood friend, my secret-keeper, my sister, who said, "Why so skinny, Sister?" Then something so strange and nice happened—for the first time in my entire life, Khaleq and I gave each other a hug with big smiles on our faces.

"Wow, Sister, you have abs," Khaleq said, as I was wearing a crop top. I hugged Razeq's kids—Reza, Yalda, and Amir—one by one, and we headed inside, where dinner was ready. We sat around the tablecloth once again, me and my family.

That night, we stayed up until 4 a.m. I looked so carefully at everyone. I found new and old wrinkles on Nana's face, but she looked happier than her younger self.

"Is America very different from here?" Nana asked and was surprised when I told her not at all—there were just fewer buildings in Canada. Razeq's kids were so goofy, keeping me entertained all morning with their funny stories from high school and their struggles with learning English.

"Do you like Canada, Nana?" I asked.

"I often feared going to an infidel land, and now I feel safer and more protected here than being with my whole people. It is nice, but sometimes I miss your siblings." I took my phone and called the family group, where Latif, Aziz, Razeq, Naser, and Zaher joined us from Iran, where they had been before the fall of Afghanistan. I wished they could have been in Herat when Nana, Zia, Khaleq, and the kids got on the plane, but I was so happy to know that they felt content where they were now. "I hope to see you guys too," I said on the call and promised Fadia to bring her for a visit soon.

Nana made me incredibly happy. Finally, she was optimistic about our future—and about us kids. Khaleq was already working as a professional hairdresser in Canada. Nana was also making progress; she knew her A-B-Cs and could count from one to three in English. She had a little whiteboard where she practiced her alphabet, so she could navigate Canada using buses and read numbers.

A few weeks later, I was preparing for my biggest performance yet—at the presentation of the Freedom Prize in Normandy, France. Like everyone else, Nana was thrilled that I would be performing in front of four thousand people and that she would see my performance for the first time.

A few days before the event, Nana said, "I have something for you." She had designed and made a custom outfit for me to wear during my performance—a blazer with gold embroidery on both sides, making me look bold and striking.

"I love this!" I exclaimed. I hugged Nana, not just because I had something special to wear, but because she, who had once been against my rapping, was now my biggest fan.

"I love you!" I told Nana, sharing a sentiment I hadn't dared to express years ago.

She surprised me by finally saying the words I had been waiting for: "I love you too, and I am proud of you."

My family, reunited.

Acknowledgments

It took me several years to prepare this book, both for myself and for you. Crafting a detailed memoir that offers something meaningful came with both laughter and shattering tears. I am grateful that I put everything on paper, and I want to take this moment to thank those who gave me love, support, and guidance in completing my memoir.

Thank you to Rokhsareh Ghaemmaghami, Mrs. Farzaneh Poori, Sohaila Yazdani, and the rest of the Khaneh Meher NGO who first believed in me. To Joe Loftin, for granting me access to education. To Cori Stern, Laurie Michaels, and Zoe Adams, for trusting my voice and supporting me through this journey. To my American family, for providing the mental strength I needed. To Leon Botstein, president of Bard College, and to all Bard faculty, especially to Gilles Peress and my college advisor, Roger Berkowitz. To Deborah Maine and Sarah Robbins for their support in developing my writing skills. To Mark Tauber, for recognizing the importance of sharing this story. Thanks to Elizabeth Rubin, and to Angela Guzman.

And my heartfelt thanks to all of my lifelong friends especially Feri and Meri, for being by my side, and to my mother, for her love and support. I thank you all for shaping my story.

Further Listening

I wrote three original pieces of music and included "Daughters for Sale," one of my older songs, in this book to add a touch of my heart and express what I would have said through music. I've included the chapters that each song best coincides with. Scan the QR code or visit sonita.net/book to listen.

1. Chapter 1: "Go Away, War"
2. Chapter 3: "My Heart Is Yours"
3. Chapter 17: "Daughters for Sale"
4. Chapter 20: "Human Rights Is a Brand"

Author's Note

This is a work of nonfiction. The events and experiences detailed herein are all true and have been faithfully rendered as I have remembered them, to the best of my ability. Some names, identities, and circumstances have been changed in order to protect the anonymity of the various individuals involved. Conversations are not written to represent word-for-word documentation; rather, I've retold them in a way that evokes the real feeling and meaning of what was said, in keeping with the true essence of the mood and spirit of the events.

About the Author

Sonita Alizada is the first professional Afghan rapper, a human rights activist, and an author. She is the cofounder of Arezo and the Dreams Book, a secret school for Afghan girls deprived of education. Born under Taliban rule, she faced the threat of child marriage twice, at ages ten and sixteen, before finding her voice through music. Her rap video for "Daughters for Sale" gained international recognition, amplifying her fight against child marriage. Her story was documented in the Sundance Film Festival award-winning film *Sonita.* A Global Rhodes Scholar, she has received numerous accolades, including MTV Europe's Generation Change Award, the Freedom Prize, the Cannes Lions Award, and a place on Forbes 30 Under 30.